pathfinder guide

Surrey and Sussex

WALKS

Compiled by
John Brooks,
Brian Conduit and
Kevin Borman

JARROLD
publishing

D0995129

Acknowledgements

We are grateful for the advice and assistance of Mr S. Diserens (East Sussex County Council), Mr R. Blatchford (Surrey County Council), Mr E.M. Holdsworth (West Sussex County Council) and Paula Eatough (National Trust, Southern Region). We also extend special thanks to Mrs J.M. Barber of Horsham, Mr V.L. Cole of Farnham, Mrs Nancy Etherton and Mr Alan Wilmshurst of Crowborough, Dr B.J. Goldsmith of Horley and Mr D.K. Johnson of Goring-by-Sea, all members of the Ramblers' Association who have provided valuable assistance in checking changes to routes.

Text:	Brian Conduit, John Brooks and Kevin Borman
Photography:	Jarrold Publishing
Editor:	Sonya Calton
Designers:	Brian Skinner, Doug Whitworth
Series Consultant:	Brian Conduit

Jarrold Publishing   ISBN 0-7117-0610-7

While every care has been taken to ensure the accuracy of the route directions, the publishers cannot accept responsibility for errors or omissions, or for changes in details given. The countryside is not static: hedges and fences can be removed, field boundaries can alter, footpaths can be rerouted and changes in ownership can result in the closure or diversion of some concessionary paths. Also, paths that are easy and pleasant for walking in fine conditions may become slippery, muddy and difficult in wet weather, while stepping stones across rivers and streams may become impassable.

If you find an inaccuracy in either the text or maps, please write or e-mail to Jarrold Publishing at the addresses below.

First published 1993
Revised and reprinted 1997, 2000 and 2003

Printed in Belgium by Proost NV, Turnhout. 5/03

Jarrold Publishing
Pathfinder Guides, Whitefriars, Norwich NR3 1TR
E-mail: info@totalwalking.co.uk
www.totalwalking.co.uk

Front cover: Bateman's, Burwash
Previous page: Old Town, Hastings

Contents

The National Trust; The Ramblers' Association; Walkers and the Law; Countryside Access Charter; Walking Safety; Useful Organisations; Ordnance Survey Maps

■ Short, easy walks

■ Walks of modest length, likely to involve some modest uphill walking

■ More challenging walks which may be longer and/or over more rugged terrain, often with some stiff climbs

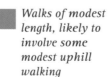

Keymap 1

GUILDFORD

ALDERSHOT

GODALMING

HASLEMERE

BORDON

Liphook

Hindhead

Grayshott
Shottermill

Camelsdale

Midhurst

Petworth

Pulbor

ARUNDEL

CHICHESTER

Bosham

Southbourne

BOGNOR REGIS

LITTLEHAMP

SOUTH DOWNS

Keymap 2

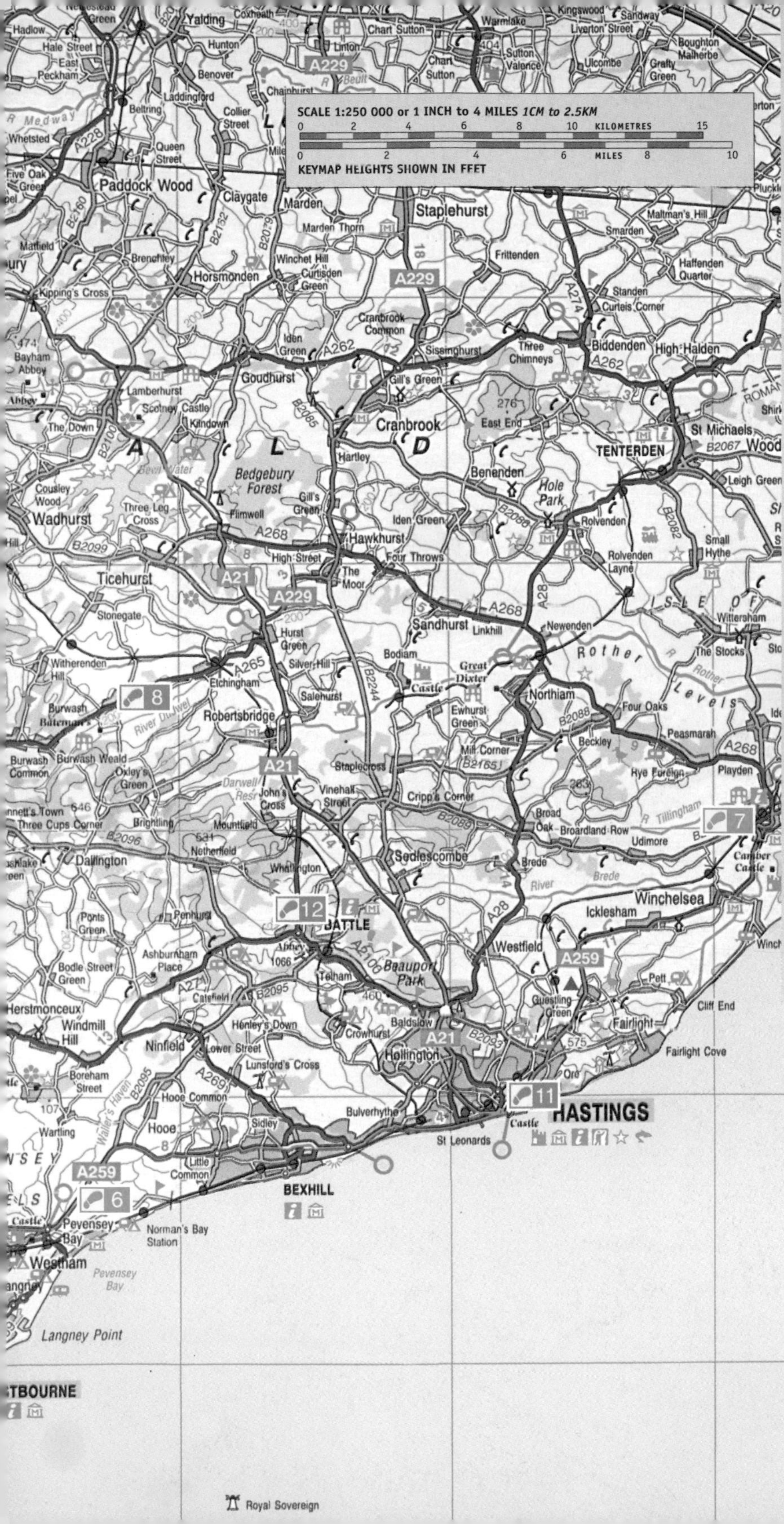

SCALE 1:250 000 or 1 INCH to 4 MILES *1CM to 2.5KM*

0 2 4 6 8 10 KILOMETRES 15

0 2 4 6 MILES 8 10

KEYMAP HEIGHTS SHOWN IN FEET

A229 • A262 • A268 • A21 • A265 • A259 • A28 • A259

TENTERDEN

HASTINGS

BEXHILL

BATTLE

Cranbrook • Goudhurst • Hawkhurst • Staplehurst • Horsmonden • Wadhurst • Ticehurst • Robertsbridge • Sedlescombe • Winchelsea • Westfield • Fairlight • Pevensey Bay • Westham

Paddock Wood • Benenden • Biddenden • High Halden • St Michaels • Rolvenden • Northiam • Peasmarsh • Playden

Royal Sovereign

At-a-glance...

Walk	Page	Start	Distance	Time
Albury Downs and St Martha's Hill	51	Newlands Corner	7 miles (11.3km)	3½ hrs
Alfriston, Long Man of Wilmington and Jevington	66	Alfriston	8 miles (12.9km)	4 hrs
Arundel Park and South Stoke	59	Arundel	7 miles (11.3km)	3½ hrs
Ashdown Forest	56	Gills Gap	6½ miles (10.5km)	3½ hrs
Battle	40	Battle	6 miles (9.7km)	3½ hrs
Bignor Hill and Stane Street	72	Bignor Hill	8 miles (12.9km)	4 hrs
Bosham and Fishbourne	43	Bosham	8½ miles (13.7km)	4½ hrs
Box Hill, Ranmore Common, Norbury Park ...	69	Box Hill	11 miles (17.7km)	5 hrs
Burwash and Bateman's	30	Burwash	5 miles (8km)	2½ hrs
Cissbury and Chanctonbury Rings	87	Findon Valley	10½ miles (16.9km)	5½ hrs
Cranleigh	22	Cranleigh	5 miles (8km)	2½ hrs
Devil's Dyke	18	Devil's Dyke Hotel	3½ miles (5.6km)	2½ hrs
The Devil's Punchbowl	46	Hindhead	5½ miles (8.9km)	3 hrs
Ditchling Beacon and Wolstonbury Hill	81	Ditchling Beacon	9½ miles (15.3km)	4 hrs
Frensham Common and Kettlebury Hill	84	Frensham Little Pond	8 miles (12.9km)	4 hrs
Friston Forest, the Seven Sisters and Cuckmere	78	Exceat	6½ miles (10.5km)	3½ hrs
Hambledon, Hascombe and the Hurtwood	54	Hambledon	6½ miles (10.5km)	3 hrs
Hartfield, Withyham and '500' Acre Wood	32	Hartfield	6 miles (9.7km)	3 hrs
Hastings Country Park	38	Hastings Old Town	5 miles (8km)	2½ hrs
Kingley Vale	16	West Stoke	3½ miles (5.6km)	2 hrs
Leith Hill and Friday Street	48	Coldharbour	6½ miles (10.5km)	3½ hrs
Lewes, Balmer Down and the River Ouse	75	Lewes	10 miles (16km)	5 hrs
Midhurst and Cowdray Park	35	Midhurst	6½ miles (10.5km)	3 hrs
Pevensey Levels	24	Pevensey	5 miles (8km)	3 hrs
Reigate and Colley Hills	20	Reigate Hill	3½ miles (5.6km)	2 hrs
Rye and Winchelsea	27	Rye	5½ miles (8.9km)	2½ hrs
St Leonard's Forest	14	Mannings Heath	4 miles (6.4km)	2 hrs
Wisborough Green, Arun valley and the Mens	62	Wisborough Green	9½ miles (15.3km)	5 hrs

Comments

Both at the start on the Albury Downs and from St Martha's Church, the highest points on the walk, there are superb views over the North Downs and Weald.

A grand scenic walk on the South Downs that gives fine views of the Long Man of Wilmington, an ancient and intriguing chalk figure.

The outward route lies through the splendid park of Arundel Castle while the return follows the meanderings of the River Arun, which provides a fine foreground for views of the romantic stronghold.

Most of the route is across the open heathland of Ashdown Forest, the last remaining area of wilderness in south-east England.

The highlight here is the short stretch along Wadhurst Lane, formerly used by packhorses and retaining its medieval flavour with a canopy of boughs masking the sky.

There are superb views over the South Downs all the way, especially on the final part of the walk that follows the line of a Roman road across the downs.

Ornithologists will find constant interest in this walk which takes in two estuaries, favourite haunts for waders and other over-wintering species. The lovely little church at Apuldram should not be missed.

The walk opens with the spectacular view from Box Hill, yet there is no anticlimax in what follows. There are steep gradients, and the way can be muddy so allow adequate time and take refreshments.

Holton Lane on the outward section is used by horses and may be muddy. This is the only drawback to a walk that encompasses the countryside surrounding Bateman's, once the home of Rudyard Kipling.

Plenty of open and exhilarating walking across the South Downs, with visits to two impressive prehistoric hill-forts.

The route has no taxing gradient as it winds through meadows to a disused canal tow-path (beware of rampant nettles and brambles). The final section is also level, following an abandoned railway.

An excellent introduction to a popular area, this walk begins with a steep descent and ends with a demanding climb. In between the way lies on field paths that skirt two attractive villages.

This upland walk follows the rim of the Devil's Punchbowl. The outward part is through woodland, and the return climbs to sandy heathland and the summit of Gibbet Hill.

Ditchling Beacon is a popular viewpoint as cars can be driven almost to the top. Wolstonbury Hill is remote and much less visited, and in between the walk covers miles of beautiful downland countryside.

Pines of Frensham Common contribute to a landscape that could belong to Scotland, while in contrast the ridge of Kettlebury Hill provides excellent walking with views extending over much of Surrey.

A varied walk through forest, across downland, along cliffs and by a river estuary. The most spectacular stretch is across the chalk cliffs of the Seven Sisters.

The route traverses large tracts of woodland that often screen long vistas but there are excellent views from Hydon's Ball and Vann Hill, and both Hambledon and Hascombe are villages of rare character.

A walk in the 'Winnie the Pooh Country' of Ashdown Forest, going through part of Five Hundred Acre Wood and crossing 'Pooh Bridge'.

A splendid walk along the spectacular cliffs and through the wooded inland glens that lie to the east of Hastings.

Much of this walk follows a trail around what is alleged to be the finest remaining yew forest in Europe.

A woodland and heathland walk that climbs to the highest point in south-east England, a magnificent vantage-point over the Weald.

The route winds through historic Lewes at the start but soon climbs to the Downs and follows the South Downs Way northwards across lonely countryside before turning away to the west to Offham.

Mainly level – but never dull – walking takes you through woodland and the parkland surrounding the great Tudor palace of Cowdray, which has stood in ruins since a fire in 1793.

The Pevensey Levels are in low-lying pastures where it is difficult to avoid cattle. The brave walker will be rewarded by lonely, beautiful countryside, which is a delight to botanists and birdwatchers.

The first half of this well-wooded walk is along the ridge of the North Downs; the second half follows the Pilgrims' Ways along the base of that ridge.

Two of the medieval Cinque Ports, both fascinating towns, are linked by this walk across marshes reclaimed from the retreating sea.

A short and pleasant walk through woodland that passes one of the many hammer ponds of the Sussex Weald.

This walk in the flat country of the Low Weald, by the River Arun and disused Arun Canal, passes through some of the surviving woods of the ancient Wealden Forest.

At-a-glance...

Introduction to Surrey and Sussex

A common image of Surrey and Sussex today is that they are the quintessential commuter counties: affluent, over-populated and criss-crossed by busy railway lines and congested roads radiating from London. In this view, a diminishing amount of countryside is being gradually engulfed by a rising tide of bricks, concrete and tarmac. As is so often the case, the image does not match the reality and a number of popular misconceptions about the region need to be eliminated.

First, despite the area's proximity to London, the M25 and Heathrow and Gatwick airports, there is perhaps a surprising amount of open, unspoilt and varied countryside left. Indeed, walkers in many parts of the region may find themselves treading some of the quietest and loneliest footpaths in southern England.

Second, although far removed from the areas of traditional heavy industry, this was once England's major iron-producing area, the 'Black Country' of the Tudor and Stuart eras. Absence of local coal resources meant that the Industrial Revolution passed it by and little remains of its earlier industrial heritage, apart from some fine ironmasters' houses, including Rudyard Kipling's former home at Bateman's, and the numerous hammer ponds that are scattered throughout the Surrey and Sussex Weald.

Third, for an area lying between the capital and the south coast noted for its prosperity and extensive communications network, it is hard to believe that it was once wild and remote. *Weald* actually means 'wild', and the region was largely cut off from the rest of the country by thick forest and rough heath. Because of this Sussex was the last of the Saxon kingdoms to be converted to Christianity, and until the present century Surrey's infertile sandy heathlands made it one of the poorest counties in England. It is noticeable that neither Surrey nor Sussex possess the imposing medieval churches to be found in the Cotswolds, Somerset, East Anglia or the East Midlands. Even Chichester Cathedral, the finest church in the region, is not among the largest or most outstanding of English cathedrals.

The dominant geographical features, stretching like two fingers across Surrey and Sussex from west to east, are the North and South Downs, whose steepest escarpments look inward over the Weald that they encompass. The North Downs belong to Surrey, their slopes more extensively covered with trees than those of the south. Although well-wooded in parts, especially in the west, the South Downs exhibit all the finest characteristics of chalk downland scenery. With smooth and rolling contours, short and springy sheep-cropped turf and open vistas, they sweep across Sussex to terminate at Beachy Head and the spectacular Seven Sisters cliffs west of Eastbourne.

Between the downs lies the Weald, a complex and scenically varied area of sandstone and clay, once covered by the vast, ancient forest of Andredesweald. A few miles to the south of the North Downs in Surrey the heavily wooded greensand ridge rises to 965ft (294m) at Leith Hill, the highest point in south-east England. In Sussex the sandstone uplands of the High Weald reach up to 732ft (223m) amid the scattered birch, pine and open heathland of Ashdown Forest, and meet the English Channel to the east of Hastings, producing some of the finest cliff scenery on the south coast. From the many high vantage points, grand views extend across the flatter, clay lands of the Low Weald; here is what many would claim to be the archetypal Wealden landscape of wide vistas, lazily meandering rivers, farms, woodland and idyllic villages of tile-hung houses and spacious greens.

Apart from the chalk cliffs where the South Downs meet the sea and the sandstone cliffs near Hastings, the Sussex coast is fairly flat. A combination of easy access to London and a relatively dry and warm climate gave rise to some of England's earliest and best-known holiday resorts. However, outside the built-up areas can be found an atmospheric and often haunting landscape of lonely marshlands, winding creeks and distant horizons, frequented more by the naturalist and ornithologist but not to be ignored by the walker, whose first thought might be to head for the downs. Walks among these coastal lowlands around Chichester harbour, across the Pevensey Levels and over the reclaimed marshes near Rye are featured, as well as more energetic and dramatic cliff walks in the Seven Sisters and Hastings country parks.

Prehistoric settlers were more attracted to the drier slopes of the South Downs than the damp clays and impenetrable forests of the Weald, and some fine prehistoric monuments survive here. Largest and most impressive of these is Cissbury Ring to the north of Worthing, one of the most extensive Iron Age forts in the country, with grand views over both downs and coast. The Romans also favoured the downs and built a number of villas on the sunny, south-facing slopes. They established Chichester as their headquarters and built a road across Sussex and Surrey to link it with London; parts of this route (Stane Street) have been converted into modern roads but some sections survive as a footpath, especially the highly attractive

Looking down over the Weald from Gills Lap – one of the highest viewpoints in Ashdown Forest

and scenic stretch that climbs from near Eartham on to the crest of the South Downs at Bignor Hill.

The most constant historic theme of this area has been the threat of invasion from across the Channel, and throughout the region there are many reminders of this threat from the Roman period onwards. As Roman power dwindled and Anglo-Saxon attacks on the English coast intensified, the Romans built a chain of forts, 'Forts of the Saxon Shore', in an attempt to keep the invaders at bay. An outstanding example is to be found at Pevensey, part of which was later incorporated into a Norman castle. The forts, however, were a failure; the Saxons penetrated the region and created Sussex, or 'kingdom of the South Saxons'.

Sussex witnessed the best-known and indeed the last successful invasion of England in 1066 and both Hastings Castle, which William the Conqueror ordered to be constructed while waiting to do battle, and Battle Abbey, on the site of the decisive encounter itself, are reminders of the Norman Conquest. To consolidate their conquest and protect this highly vulnerable region between London and the south coast, the Normans built a

The tranquil surroundings of Juniper Bottom

series of castles at strategic locations on the main river-routes, as at Arundel, Lewes, Bramber, Farnham and Guildford. Constant wars or threats of war between England and France caused later medieval monarchs to create the federation of the Cinque Ports – five (later seven) towns on the Kent and Sussex coasts entrusted with the task of providing men and ships for the defence of the Channel in return for certain privileges. Hastings, Winchelsea and Rye were among the members.

A threatened invasion in the 1530s produced the series of artillery forts built by Henry VIII, an example of which survives at Camber, near Rye. Another invasion scare, from Napoleon in the early 19th century, led to the construction both of the Royal Military Canal and a chain of martello towers; several examples of the latter can be found along the Sussex coast, including a well-preserved one on the seafront at Eastbourne.

Prosperity came to the area with the rise of the Wealden iron industry (at its height in the 16th and 17th centuries) and improvements in farming; many fine manor houses were built at this time. As charcoal was used in the smelting of iron, it was the iron industry that was responsible for the destruction of much of the Weald's extensive forest. By the 18th century a growing shortage of timber, plus the development of coke- instead of charcoal-smelting, caused the iron industry to move away to the coalfields of the Midlands and north. Thus the remaining woodlands were saved and the area was spared the environmental consequences of the Industrial Revolution. Today Surrey and Sussex have some of the most extensive tree cover of any of England's counties.

A major development in the late 18th and 19th centuries was the growth of seaside resorts. Brighton was the first, made fashionable by the Prince Regent's dalliances with his mistress there, and was followed by Eastbourne, Hastings and Worthing. The initial trickle of aristocratic visitors later became a torrent as the building of railways between these resorts and London brought increasing numbers of middle- and working-class holidaymakers to enjoy the delights of 'Sussex by the sea'.

It was the railways, and later the roads, that brought about the greatest transformation of all, making it possible for much of the region to become a desirable commuter area for people working in London. In particular Surrey was turned from a poor, rural backwater into the busy, prosperous and heavily-populated county of today. Many of the villages and smaller towns of the region, that had remained essentially unspoilt because of the absence of large-scale development in the Victorian period, owe their present neat and well-ordered appearance to the new lease of life given them by an influx of 20th-century commuter affluence. It is to be hoped that future population and commercial pressures do not harm the qualities of the area that both inhabitants and visitors find so appealing.

For the walker, the area has many attractions. There is a wide variety of terrain, ranging from the open ridge-tops of the North and South Downs to the creeks and marshes around Chichester harbour, from the tree-clad slopes of the greensand ridge to the dramatic cliffs near Hastings, and from the wild heathland of Ashdown Forest to the gentle river valleys of the Low Weald. Surrey and Sussex have some of the densest networks of public footpaths and bridleways in the country, supplemented by country parks and the extensive possessions of the National Trust in the area. There can be no other part of England that is criss-crossed by more long-distance and recreational paths. Foremost among these are the national trails of the North Downs Way and South Downs Way, but in addition there are the Greensand Way, Wealdway, Vanguard Way, Sussex Border Path, Downs Link and Wey-South Path. Footpaths are generally well-maintained and well-waymarked to aid route-finding.

Note on South Downs National Park: The Countryside Agency, the government body responsible for national parks, organised a period of public consultation on the proposed boundaries of the South Downs National Park between November 2001 and February 2002. Consultations with local authorities took place between May and August 2002 and at the time of publication of this edition an announcement of a public inquiry was imminent. A final announcement on the establishment of the South Downs National Park is still, therefore, some way off.

St Leonard's Forest

Start	Forestry Commission's Roosthole car park, on minor road about 2 miles (3.2km) east of Horsham and 1 mile (1.6km) north of Mannings Heath
Distance	4 miles (6.4km)
Approximate time	2 hours
Parking	Roosthole car park
Refreshments	None
Ordnance Survey maps	Landranger 187 (Dorking, Reigate & Crawley), Explorer 134 (Crawley & Horsham)

St Leonard's Forest lies between Horsham and Crawley and in the Middle Ages was one of a series of adjacent, thickly wooded areas that occupied the 'Forest Ridge' of the Sussex Weald. Nowadays it is a pleasant mixture of conifer and broad-leaved woodland, farmland and heathland, which are all included in this easy walk, as is one of the ubiquitous hammer ponds, a reflection of the past importance of the iron industry in this area.

In the early 19th century William Cobbett described St Leonard's Forest as a 'miserable tract of heath and fern and bushes and sand'. It was the demand for charcoal from the local ironmasters that led to the felling of much of the forest, especially during the 16th and 17th centuries at the height of the Wealden iron industry, but some traditional woodland survives, considerably augmented by the more recent conifer plantations of the Forestry Commission. The forest is thought to get its name from a former chapel within it, dedicated to St Leonard.

From the car park turn left along the road for ¼ mile (400m) and turn down the first lane on the right **Ⓐ**, signposted to Mannings Heath. The lane

heads gently downhill. At a left-hand bend turn right over a stile **Ⓑ**, at a public footpath sign, to follow a path across a field, soon curving left to keep alongside a wire fence on the right to another stile. Climb it, entering the woodlands of Alder Copse, and keep along the inside left-hand edge of the wood to Roosthole Pond. This

---

Roosthole Pond in St Leonard's Forest

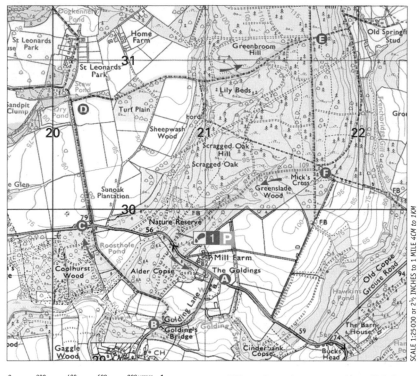

SCALE 1:25000 or 2½ INCHES to 1 MILE 4CM to 1KM

is one of the numerous hammer ponds in the forest; the overflow from them provided the power for the hammers used in the iron industry.

Cross the end of the pond, continue gently uphill, now along the inside right-hand edge of Coolhurst Wood, and climb a stile to rejoin the road **C**. Cross over and walk along the broad, straight, tree-lined track opposite. After ½ mile (800m) you reach a metal gate; just in front of it turn right **D**, at a footpath sign, onto a narrow path that squeezes between trees and bushes on the left and a hedge and wire fence bordering a field on the right. This path may be overgrown and awkward in places. When you have passed the end of the field bear left along an obvious and easier path across an area of rough grass and scrub, cross a track, then climb a stile at a public footpath sign and continue across an open landscape of grassland fringed by trees.

Where the path peters out bear slightly right, making for a wire fence at the field edge and keep alongside it to descend into woodland. Keep ahead at a public footpath sign and path junction – in front is a Forestry Commission sign for Lily Beds. Pass to the right of a shallow pond and continue gently uphill along a grassy track through mixed woodland. Keep a sharp look-out for a public footpath sign by a slight right-hand bend which directs you to bear left along a narrow path, still heading gently uphill. At a public footpath sign pass beside a wooden barrier to cross a track and continue across an area of heathland, past another public footpath sign and continuing to the next one at a crossing of tracks and paths **E**.

Turn right here to walk along a wide, geometrically straight track and after ½ mile (800m) you reach a public footpath sign at another crossing of tracks and paths. Keep ahead for a few yards and then turn right **F** along an attractive forest track which leads directly back to the car park. ●

Kingley Vale

Start	West Stoke – ½ mile (800m) north of B2178 at East Ashling
Distance	3½ miles (5.6km)
Approximate time	2 hours
Parking	West Stoke
Refreshments	None
Ordnance Survey maps	Landranger 197 (Chichester & The Downs), Explorer 120 (Chichester)

Kingley Vale lies below the South Downs and its thickly wooded slopes embrace the finest yew forest in Europe, now a National Nature Reserve managed and conserved by English Nature. After a short walk across open country from the village of West Stoke to reach the edge of the vale, you follow a nature trail around it, winding through dark and eerie groves of ancient and gnarled yew trees before heading up onto the open downland of Bow Hill. From the top there are fine views across the downs towards Chichester harbour and the coast. You then descend into the wooded vale again, finally retracing your steps to the start to conclude a most fascinating walk.

Ancient yews in Kingley Vale

The hamlet of West Stoke, lying in a quiet and remote setting near the foot of the downs, comprises little more than farm buildings, a large house and a small, simple church.

Begin by climbing a stile in the corner of the car park, at a public footpath sign, and walk along a fence-lined track. There are pleasant views on both sides across tree-fringed fields, and ahead the wooded slopes of Kingley Vale below Bow Hill soon come into sight.

After ¾ mile (1.2km) you arrive at a stile on the edge of the nature reserve **A**. Climb it and keep ahead, passing by the Field Museum to reach the start of the numbered nature trail. You now follow the trail in an anti-clockwise direction around the vale; there are twenty-four numbered green posts in all. The first part is particularly fascinating as you walk through groves of ancient yews – huge and gnarled trees, some of which are at least 500 years old. One legend claims that a grove was planted to commemorate a victory here against the Vikings in the 9th century. There are other trees as well, including an equally ancient and gnarled oak, and a series of information boards.

After a while the trail climbs alongside the right-hand edge of the reserve, over several stiles and by a wire fence on the right, to continue across more open grassland, curving gradually to the left to reach the top of Bow Hill, where you meet a straight track at post 18 **B**. To the right are two of the four Devil's Humps (the other two are hidden by trees) – Bronze

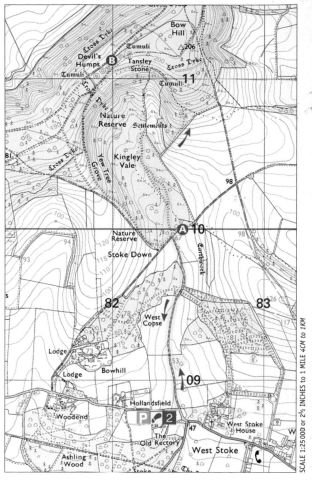

SCALE 1:25 000 or 2½ INCHES to 1 MILE 4CM to 1KM

Age tombs erected around 500 BC. It is worth while making a brief detour to them for the magnificent all-round view: westwards over the downs and eastwards to the coast and inlets of Chichester harbour.

Immediately bear left off the track along a path which re-enters woodland and passes through another dark and eerie part of the yew forest, heading gently downhill above the rim of the steep-sided, thickly wooded vale. Keep curving gradually to the left all the while, climb a stile and continue down to another stile at the edge of the nature reserve **A**. Turn right over it and retrace your steps along the track to West Stoke.

Devil's Dyke

Start	Devil's Dyke Hotel
Distance	3½ miles (5.6km)
Approximate time	2½ hours
Parking	Devil's Dyke Hotel
Refreshments	Pubs at start, Poynings and Fulking
Ordnance Survey maps	Landranger 198 (Brighton & The Downs), Explorer 122 (South Downs Way – Steyning to Newhaven)

Starting from one of southern England's finest viewpoints, the rest of this walk continues in the same vein. The climb back to the ridge at the end is an exhilarating finale to a route which combines the best features of downland- and field-walking, as well as visiting two charming villages.

On a fine day you may have to arrive early to find a place in the car park at the Devil's Dyke Hotel. The spectacular view makes this a popular venue, and its airiness attracts kite-flyers. With your back to the hotel, turn right and walk past the large stone memorial seat (which dates from 1928 when the Dyke estate was given to the nation), continuing in a north-easterly direction along the crest of the ridge. Ignore a stile on the left which

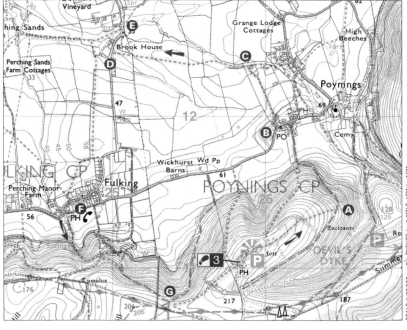

SCALE 1:25000 or 2½ INCHES to 1 MILE 4CM to 1KM

leads directly to Poynings and omits an attractive portion of the route.

When the path along the ridge comes to a stile, climb it and descend to another path below **Ⓐ** which follows a ledge. Turn left onto this bridleway and follow it northwards to a beautiful wood, where it begins to descend more steeply and can become very muddy after wet weather. The subsequent level path into Poynings can also be muddy. When

The fine panorama from Devil's Dyke

this path reaches the main street, turn right if you wish to visit the pub, otherwise turn left and pass the post office. On the apex of the following bend look for a footpath sign on the right that points into a short lane **Ⓑ**. This leads to a gate, which opens into a long meadow. Go ahead on a path and at the far end of the meadow go through a gate to join a track.

Turn left after the stile **Ⓒ** onto an attractive path running along the bank of a stream that flows through two ponds. After these, cross the stream by a bridge and then make for another stile on the far side of a meadow. A second meadow follows, crossed by a sunken field path. Continue straight across the next large field – this is enjoyable walking with a fine view of the Devil's Dyke ridge to the left and rolling countryside ahead and to the right. Cross the small field that follows to reach a lane **Ⓓ**.

Turn right and follow the lane for 250 yds (228m) before turning left immediately after a small bridge **Ⓔ**. Go over the stile by the side of a concrete drive signposted 'Brookside'. A short, rather overgrown stretch leads to a stile into a field. Here the going is easier, with the sound of running water on the left. Climb the stile leading out of the

field, then cross a bridge and another stile, and walk 50 yds (45m) by a stream to find a bridge over it on the left. Cross this and follow a field path heading south. The path runs along the right-hand side of a succession of fields, crossing a farm track at one point. At the end of the field nearest the houses, after a stile, pass through a kissing-gate on the right.

Take the left edge of the field for about 50 yds (45m), then bear diagonally left across an arable field, making for the right hand end of a brick wall largely hidden by vegetation. Climb a few steps to a kissing-gate, then follow the left edge of a small paddock to reach the road through Fulking.

Turn right down the lane, and directly before the pub there is a bridleway on the left **Ⓕ**. Take this and after 50 yds (45m) look for steps up the bank on the right, from which a footpath leads off. This footpath provides walkers with a taxing climb up the Fulking escarpment before open downland is reached. Keep straight on where five footpaths cross **Ⓖ**, and after this junction the Devil's Dyke Hotel comes into sight ahead. ●

Reigate and Colley Hills

Start	Top of Reigate Hill
Distance	3½ miles (5.6km)
Approximate time	2 hours
Parking	Reigate Hill
Refreshments	Refreshment kiosk on Reigate Hill
Ordnance Survey maps	Landranger 187 (Dorking, Reigate & Crawley), Explorer 146 (Dorking, Box Hill & Reigate)

*This walk follows a straightforward 'across-down-across-up'
pattern. Starting from the top of Reigate Hill you follow the
ridge of the North Downs – well-wooded but with some grand
views – across the adjacent Reigate and Colley Hills, both
National Trust properties, before descending and then
continuing along the base of them, following the Pilgrims' Way
through woodland. The only part of the route that is quite
strenuous comes near the end: a steep climb up a rather
narrow and overgrown path to regain the top of Reigate Hill.
On the first part of the walk along the ridge, the M25 is
immediately below on the right – fortunately out of sight if not
out of hearing.*

Begin by walking past the refreshment
kiosk and toilet block to cross a footbridge
over the main road and continue along a
wooded track, from which there are fine
views to the left over Reigate. On meeting
a tarmac drive keep ahead along it – after

the last of the houses it becomes a rough
track – and pass between Reigate Fort on
the left and a water tower on the right to

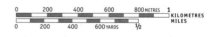

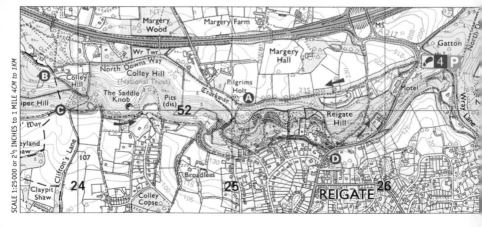

View from Reigate Hill

woodland; a gap in the trees reveals a superb view to the right over the Surrey countryside. The path curves to the right and continues down to a crossing of paths. Turn left here **C**, through a wooden barrier with a yellow waymark, to leave the North Downs Way and join the Pilgrims' Way.

Now keep along a most attractive wooded path that winds and undulates along the base of first Colley and later Reigate Hill, initially passing some fine old yews. At a fork keep ahead along the right-hand path to go down steps, bear left at the bottom of them, go down a few more steps to a T-junction and then bear left. Continue along the base of Reigate Hill, curving right at one point, eventually passing beside a barrier and a National Trust Pilgrims' Way sign onto a tarmac lane.

Keep ahead for about 100 yds (91m) and where the lane bends to the right, bear left along a track at a bridleway sign, initially between walls on both sides, still along the base of Reigate Hill. Continue between houses on the edge of Reigate to emerge onto the main road, turn left and after a few yards bear left **D**, signposted Public Highway, to follow a narrow, enclosed, sunken and likely to be overgrown path steeply uphill. Near the top keep by a wooden fence on the right; after passing Rock Farm the path broadens into a clear and unobstructed track which continues up to a tarmac drive by a bend.

Turn right, at a North Downs Way sign, along a track and retrace your steps to the start. ●

enter the National Trust property of Reigate Hill. Continue along the beautifully wooded track, passing some fine old trees, to reach the circular, classical-style pavilion on Colley Hill, on which an inscription reads 'Presented to the Corporation of the Borough of Reigate for the Benefit of the Public by Lieutenant-Colonel Robert William Inglis in 1909' **A**. This is a magnificent viewpoint, looking along the ridge of the North Downs to Box Hill and across to Leith Hill and the greensand ridge. A toposcope indicates the features that can be seen from here.

Continue over Colley Hill, still following a tree-lined track. At a fork pass through a wooden barrier to continue along the left-hand track, by a fence on the left, and pass through a second wooden barrier onto a tarmac drive **B**. Turn left in front of a gate and fence and then turn left again along an enclosed path that heads steeply downhill through

Cranleigh

Start	Cranleigh
Distance	5 miles (8km)
Approximate time	2½ hours
Parking	Cranleigh – main car park almost opposite church
Refreshments	Pubs in Cranleigh
Ordnance Survey maps	Landrangers 186 (Aldershot & Guildford) and 187 (Dorking, Reigate & Crawley), Explorer 134 (Crawley & Horsham)

This is an easy stroll with a level course which passes through meadows, along the trackbed of the former Horsham to Guildford railway and a little-used path by the Wey and Arun Junction Canal (like the railway, also disused) to follow a cross-country track picturesquely known as Lion's Lane. However, the canalside section is likely to be overgrown and difficult in places, and in view of that it is inadvisable to wear shorts for this walk.

Leave the car park and turn left to pass Cranleigh Post Office. Turn left again opposite the Onslow Arms pub into Knowle Lane. Just beyond the drive on the left which goes to the recreation centre (and after a small bridge) climb the stile **Ⓐ** on the right onto a field path along the left side of a beautiful meadow. When this path reaches Alfold Road turn left and follow it for ¼ mile (400m) before turning right **Ⓑ** onto the drive to Uttworth Manor.

Follow this bridleway towards the attractive old house as far as the pond. The bridleway bears left here to cut off the corner of a field: head for a large ash tree on the right-hand side of the field to join a track following the edge. Before reaching the end of the field cross the deep ditch on the right by a footbridge, and follow the path below the bank of the canal which fell into disuse when the railways became established.

The bridleway has also become neglected and in places balsam, nettles and brambles threaten to engulf the path. There is dense woodland to the left and a companion waterway may be glimpsed here. Unlike the canal to the right, this one is well filled with water.

Great Garson, an attractive old manor-house near Cranleigh

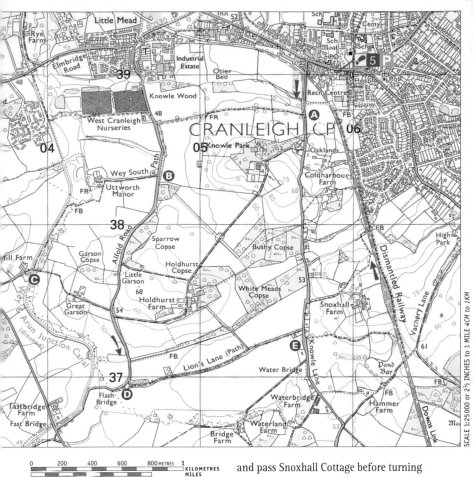

SCALE 1:25000 or 2½ INCHES to 1 MILE 4CM to 1KM

| 0 | 200 | 400 | 600 | 800 METRES | 1 |
| 0 | 200 | 400 | 600 YARDS | ½ | |

KILOMETRES
MILES

The latter is crossed by a canal bridge at Mill Farm **C**, where at a junction of bridleways our way lies to the left. The path follows the right-hand edge of two meadows to reach another old manor-house, Great Garson.

Go straight on through a wooden gate onto the drive to the house. Follow this past the pond to reach the road. Turn right, and when the road bends right take the bridleway to the left **D**, just before Flash Bridge Cottage, which winds through a small patch of woodland. This is Lion's Lane, a delightful old road which provides a mile or so of pleasant, sheltered walking.

Where this ends at a road turn left for the pub at Snoxhall, otherwise turn right and pass Snoxhall Cottage before turning left **E** and crossing a stile onto a field-edge path which leads eastwards to the dismantled railway.

Climb the embankment and turn left to begin the final leg of the walk back to Cranleigh. This is a part of the line which once ran between Horsham and Guildford. In 1922 there were seven trains in each direction on weekdays, and the journey from Cranleigh to London Bridge took just over two hours. As the path nears Cranleigh there is a concrete signalpost surmounted with the remains of a semaphore signal in the 'clear' position.

Pass a cricket-ground and by a children's playground turn right from the old railway line onto a concrete path. Turn left to cross a footbridge and then walk past tennis courts to return to the starting point.

Pevensey Levels

Start	Pevensey
Distance	5 miles (8km)
Approximate time	3 hours
Parking	Cattle Market car park by Pevensey Castle
Refreshments	Pubs at Pevensey and Westham, tearoom at Pevensey Castle
Ordnance Survey maps	Landranger 199 (Eastbourne & Hastings), Explorers 123 (South Downs Way – Newhaven to Eastbourne) and 124 (Hastings & Bexhill)

The meadowlands of the Pevensey Levels may be flat but they are seldom tedious, especially to the naturalist or ornithologist. These pastures are lonely and the landscape is dominated by the mood of the sky. This route explores footpaths and bridleways that lead through countryside largely neglected by walkers, and it is interesting to speculate on how the landscape appeared some two thousand years ago when the Romans made Pevensey a fortified gateway into Britain. A thousand years later Saxon outlaws probably used the marshlands to escape from the Norman overlords. Follow the route directions carefully: the meadows are grazed by cows and heifers, occasionally accompanied by a bull.

Walk to the bottom end of the car park and go through the gate into the recreation ground. Follow the path round to the right, below the ramparts of the castle. When the original castle was built by the Romans this land would have been under water, as it was in Norman times when the Roman sea fort was enlarged by Robert, Count of Mortain, into a substantial stronghold. Although often besieged it was never taken, and its defence-works proved useful in the Second World War when machine-gun redoubts were concealed in the walls as an answer to the threat of German invasion.

The sea once lapped against the walls of the eastern and southern perimeter of the castle, and the footpath skirts these by pretty meadows to reach the churchyard of St Mary's, Westham. The Normans set about building the church here at the same time as they started on the neighbouring castle. The church tower is squat yet powerful, a symbol of strength which, though not tall, is a distinctive landmark.

Turn left out of the churchyard onto the main road and then right into Peelings Lane, passing the village hall. Bear right when the road forks by the end of the pond. Turn right again at Castle Farm **Ⓐ**, where a small notice announces 'Beware Alsation loose', go through a metal gate leading out of the farmyard, and head straight on over the brow of the hill in the meadow ahead, towards the bypass. Just before this there is a dyke which is crossed

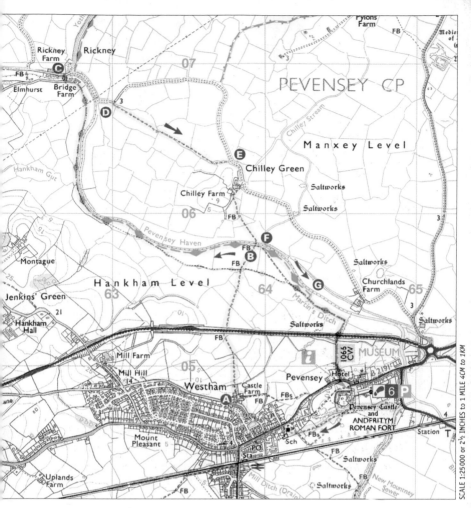

by a bridge. A stile and steps then take the path over the new road.

Once on the northern side, head directly across the meadow towards the observatory, passing through a succession of gateways. Gradually the path through the pastures becomes more discernible and eventually reaches a stile. Climb this and go slightly right across the field to a waymarked post **B**. At the post, do not cross the bridge but take the bridleway left along the south bank of Pevensey Haven. It is little use looking for breakwaters and quays here, since the river has long been closed for navigation. Instead, you may see herons or kingfishers hunting its peaceful waters.

The bridleway continues, close by the bank of the placid waterway, until a tall pylon ahead heralds the end of this pleasant section. The path skirts the left side of the farmyard at Bridge Farm to reach a quiet country lane **C**. Turn right and then immediately right again onto the road to Pevensey that crosses the river, which is now known as the Yotham. Continue down the road for nearly ½ mile (800m), passing beneath electricity cables and following the road as it bends left at a gate giving access to an angling club, and then left again. At this second corner **D** go through a gate on the right at a foot-path sign.

From here the tower of Pevensey church can be seen to the south-east and this landmark is a useful guide on the next section of the walk, over water meadows to Chilley Green.

After passing through the gate walk a few paces to the left, go through another gate and head diagonally across the meadow. There is a stile and footbridge by a clump of bushes on the far side. After crossing a ditch turn right to walk along its bank. This will eventually bring you to a gate on the right. Pass through this to another gate ahead, which leads into a small bottle-necked meadow. Keep the hedge on your left through this to a short track which reaches the road at Chilley Green **E**. Turn right and then right again, immediately after the farm, onto a track which leads to a modern house. The footpath leaves the track well before it reaches this house, however, passing through a gate on the left just beyond the farmyard. Cross the field to a footbridge and continue directly across the next field, heading once more for the tower of Pevensey church.

This leads to the banks of Pevensey Haven again and to a long footbridge **F** which takes the footpath over the river. Turn left after the bridge, following the bridleway along the waterside until a blue waymark on a post **G** directs you to a metal gate, from where a path leads, with a couple of twists, to the bypass. A series of gates and stiles takes the track across the busy road. Turn left when the lane ends at the castle walls to return to the starting point.

The remains of the Norman castle of Pevensey

Rye and Winchelsea

Start	Rye
Distance	5½ miles (8.9km)
Approximate time	2½ hours
Parking	Rye
Refreshments	Pubs, cafés and restaurants at Rye, pubs and cafés at Winchelsea
Ordnance Survey maps	Landranger 189 (Ashford & Romney Marsh), Explorer 125 (Romney Marsh, Rye & Winchelsea)

Constant threat of invasion from the Continent is the dominant theme of this walk across the marshes that lie between Rye and Winchelsea, two of the medieval Cinque Ports. The towns themselves, together with Camber Castle, the Royal Military Canal and a martello tower, represent different reactions to invasion threats in the medieval, Tudor and Napoleonic eras. This is an easy walk across flat, fresh and open marshland, an extension of the larger Romney Marsh across the Kent border, but do keep a sharp look-out for half hidden drainage channels on the first part of the walk; these are not always obvious and are potentially dangerous. Also, leave plenty of time to explore Rye and Winchelsea, two outstandingly attractive and fascinating towns.

As the title implies, the Cinque Ports were originally a confederation of five towns on the coast of Kent and Sussex. Their role was to provide ships and men for the defence of this highly vulnerable stretch of the English Channel in return for certain privileges. Rye and Winchelsea were later additions to the original five ports in the 14th century.

Rye occupies a hilltop site overlooking marshland, and the spire of its splendid, solid-looking church, despite being of the usual short and squat Sussex variety, dominates the surrounding countryside. Rye was an important and prosperous port in the Middle Ages, but its prosperity declined as the sea retreated, leaving behind one of the most delightful and

unspoilt small towns in the country. Narrow cobbled streets of timber-fronted and tiled houses, shops and inns climb from the River Rother to the medieval church and Ypres Tower, and from many different points in the town there are extensive views across the reclaimed marshes to the sea, now 2 miles (3.2km) away. Mermaid Street is the most photogenic and best-known street but there are lots of other old streets, alleys and attractive little squares to explore. Rye is not just a museum piece, however; there is plenty of bustle and there are still fishing vessels and boat-building yards down by the river.

The walk starts at Strand Quay by the bridge over the River Rother. Cross the

SCALE 1:25000 or 2½ INCHES to 1 MILE 4CM to 1KM

```
0      200    400    600    800 METRES  1
                                        KILOMETRES
0      200    400    600 YARDS   ½      MILES
```

bridge, walk along New Winchelsea Road and after a few yards turn right along a track, at a public footpath sign to Winchelsea. The track passes to the right of a farm, bends to the left and finishes in front of a metal gate. Go through the gate and keep straight ahead across a field to pass through two more metal gates in quick succession at the far end.

Follow the narrow but generally distinct and certainly well-waymarked path to Winchelsea, which is in sight on the wooded cliff ahead all the time, across flat fields and sheep pastures reclaimed from the sea. It is very important initially to keep to the left of a drainage channel, otherwise you will stray off the route and could easily fall into one of the numerous half-hidden channels. Indeed, for much of the way you keep along the left bank of a drainage channel, but look out for where yellow waymarks and footpath signs show deviations from a generally straight line and direct you over a number of stiles and footbridges. All around are wide, open views: Winchelsea ahead, Rye on its hill behind, low hills to the right and flat marshes looking towards the coast on the left. Finally, the path bears right and heads across to a stile by a bridge **A**.

Climb the stile, turn left to cross the

bridge over the River Brede and walk along a lane to the main road where it bends sharply at the bottom of the hill on which Winchelsea stands. Turn left along the road for $\frac{1}{4}$ mile (400m) (there is a path) and look out for a flight of steps and a public footpath sign on the right **B**; the steps enable you to climb the steep, wooded cliff into Winchelsea. At the top of the steps turn right onto a narrow tarmac path and continue along a picturesque road of tile-hung cottages to a crossroads. The main part of the town is to the right.

Despite the obvious similarities between Rye and Winchelsea there are a number of differences. Winchelsea is smaller and quieter, more of a fossilised backwater, yet at the same time built on more spacious and symmetrical lines. This is because Winchelsea was built as a new town, commissioned by Edward I when Old Winchelsea was destroyed by storms in the 13th century, and it is laid out in a grid-iron pattern, a rare example of a planned medieval town. It was conceived on a large scale, intended to be the chief port for the flourishing French wine trade, but a combination of French raids and the receding of the sea meant that these grandiose ambitions were never realised. The main surviving monuments to its brief heyday are three of the four original gateways, the 14th-century Court Hall and the large and imposing ruined church, the latter comprising just the east end as its nave and transepts were destroyed by the French.

At the crossroads, turn left and follow the road as it bends sharply left, passes through Strand Gate – one of Winchelsea's medieval gateways – and continues downhill. As you descend there are superb views across the marshes to Rye and the coast. At the bottom, turn right to rejoin the main road and, where it turns left, keep ahead in the direction of Winchelsea Beach to cross the Royal

Military Canal, built in 1805 as a defence against a possible Napoleonic invasion. Continue along the road for $\frac{1}{2}$ mile (800m) and, where it bends sharply to the right, keep ahead along a track **C**.

The track bends to the left; at a fork keep ahead along the left-hand concrete track. To the right Camber Castle can be seen in an isolated position on the marshes. This was an artillery fort built by Henry VIII at a time of an invasion scare in the 1530s. Where the concrete track turns right, go through a metal gate and continue along a grassy embankment raised above sheep pastures on both sides. This keeps close to the River Brede most of the time, but on two occasions bears right, away from it. On the first occasion you can make a short detour to the right, climbing a waymarked stile, if you want a closer look at Camber Castle. When the grassy track starts to bear right for the second time, keep ahead along a much narrower path by the river, go through a metal gate, then pass to the left of houses to rejoin the track and follow it to a road **D**.

Turn left over the river near its confluence with the Rother to a T-junction. Just ahead is a martello tower, one of over seventy built at the beginning of the 19th century as another defence against an anticipated French invasion, at the time of the Napoleonic Wars. Turn right to return to the start. ●

Picturesque Mermaid Street in the fascinating Cinque Port of Rye

Burwash and Bateman's

Start	Burwash
Distance	5 miles (8km)
Approximate time	2½ hours
Parking	Burwash – car park next to Bear Inn
Refreshments	Pubs and cafés at Burwash, National Trust tearoom at Bateman's
Ordnance Survey maps	Landranger 199 (Eastbourne & Hastings), Explorer 136 (The Weald, Royal Tunbridge Wells)

This walk features views over unspoilt countryside, and much of the return half is over National Trust land surrounding Rudyard Kipling's former home, Bateman's. A bridleway may be muddy.

Burwash is a most attractive village with some handsome houses and a church that retains its Norman tower. Turn right out of the car park onto the village street and then left just after the post office down the lane leading to the Rose and Crown pub and the fire station. Take the track (Ham Lane) between the fire station and a playing-field. After ½ mile (800m), just before an iron gate, turn left to an adjacent stile. Climb this and a second stile and follow an arrow across the meadow, descending to a stile at the back of barns into woodland. The clearly defined path winds through trees to another meadow. Bear right to a stile in the bottom left corner of this field, but do not climb this. Instead turn left to follow the stream and reach an iron gate in the corner of the field. Walk down the long, narrow meadow that follows and go through another iron gate at the end of this, on the right **A**. Cross the stream and climb towards Mottynsden Farm, making for the iron gate to the right of the oast house. Go through this and pass between the farmhouse and the manor to find a driveway leading right towards a modern house. Where the driveway curves right,

continue ahead on a path that ascends the bank, passes the garage and enters an orchard. Turn right and shortly turn left at the end of the orchard. Climb by the hedgerow, turning left at the top of the orchard, to find an opening **B**, which leads onto a farm track. Turn left, passing a plaque to Flight Lieutenant R.F. Rimmer, killed in action here during the Battle of Britain.

When the track meets a lane, turn left and pass Holton Farm before turning right onto a track at the side of the farm. Although muddy at times the bridleway is more often grassy and encroached by bracken and brambles. Glimpses of open countryside are the foretaste of a splendid panorama of pastoral landscape which will be enjoyed at the top of the hill. After this, the path descends gently through woodland to reach Woodlands Farm.

The bridleway passes to the right of the farm, and then on the left the bridleway joins a sunken track. This climbs and becomes narrow and overgrown. When the bridleway meets a farm track, bear left, but leave this before the top of the hill by turning left **C** to follow a further section of ancient enclosed trackway, to reach the A265 opposite Weald House

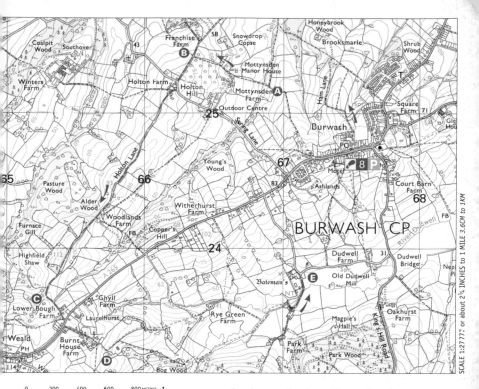

SCALE 1:27777 or about 2¼ INCHES to 1 MILE 3.6CM to 1KM

```
0    200   400   600   800 METRES  1
                                   ] KILOMETRES
                                     MILES
0    200   400   600 YARDS    ½
```

and the Burwash Weald village sign.

Turn right and walk a short distance along the main road, turning left just beyond Weald House, past concrete posts, to join the drive to Burnt House Farm. Keep straight on at the end of the drive to pass between the houses (the one on the right incorporates oast houses), making for a metal gate leading into a paddock. Go through the gate and over a stile on the left to descend to another gateway. Pass through the gateway **D** and turn left, following the yellow arrow and an iron fence. Keep to the right of this fence to a gate, pass through and continue along the fence until it ends at a stile and gateway. Cross the next field to a stile, keeping close to the hedge on the right and then walk by a few trees (pond on the right) to cross another field. Half-way across, Bateman's comes into view ahead.

The path emerges onto an asphalted drive that becomes a farm track as its heads towards a barn. The track ends at a stile, where you bear right, and walk for a short distance, keeping the hedge on the right, to reach another stile. Turn right to cross the stream and then bear left to cross the next, large field, making for the iron railings of a bridge in the fringe of trees on the far side. Cross the bridge, turn left and follow the path to a beautiful millpond, where it reaches a lane, and turn left.

The lane passes the north front of Bateman's, a fine 17th-century building Rudyard Kipling lived here until his death in 1936. At the front of the house, turn right **E** and after ¼ mile (400m) look for a stile on the left. Go over this and follow a line of old oaks to the right. Skirt the right side of a wood and from its corner go across the meadow to an old-fashioned curved stile on the far side. From here the path climbs towards Burwash. It follows the left-hand field edge, then directly crosses a field to a bridge by an oak tree. After this bear left and keep the hedge on the left until a stile is reached. Cross this to a short path back to the car park. ●

Hartfield, Withyham and Five Hundred Acre Wood

Start	Hartfield
Distance	6 miles (9.7km)
Approximate time	3 hours
Parking	Hartfield
Refreshments	Pubs at Hartfield, pub at Withyham
Ordnance Survey maps	Landranger 188 (Maidstone & The Weald of Kent), Explorer 135 (Ashdown Forest)

A.A. Milne, author of the Winnie the Pooh *books, lived near Hartfield, and this part of Ashdown Forest is the setting for many of the stories. The walk takes you through a quiet and undulating part of the forest that lies below the open heathland plateau, an attractive mixture of woodland and pasture with fine views over both the forest and the Weald. It includes two interesting village churches and crosses 'Pooh Bridge', a delightful spot in Posingford Wood where Pooh and his friends indulged in that simple but ever-popular pastime of 'Pooh-sticks'.*

Hartfield is situated on the edge of Ashdown Forest, an attractive collection of houses and cottages with a fine medieval church dominated by a 15th-century tower and broach-spire. Walk along Church Street, passing the unusual lych-gate to the churchyard on the left. Fifty yards (45m) beyond the lych-gate, directly opposite the church porch, there is a stile on the right. Climb this and turn left along the edge of the field to another stile by a metal gate. Climb the stile and continue in the same direction to climb a third stile at the far end of the field.

After this the path divides. Take the left fork to cross the field to a point where a line of oak trees – the remnants of an old hedge-line – meets the left-hand edge of the field. There is a gate and stile here and the path leads over the next field

diagonally, heading for a point to the left of Withyham church. Skirt the right-hand edge of a narrow belt of woodland and continue gently downhill to climb a stile onto a road. Turn right and cross a bridge over a stream. The village with its pub is just ahead but the route immediately turns right **A** onto a tarmac drive – signposted for Withyham church – that heads uphill, passing to the right of the church and a large house. Withyham's 14th-century church was largely rebuilt following destruction by lightning in 1663. Inside there are monuments to the Sackville family, earls and dukes of Dorset, formerly the keepers and later the owners of Ashdown Forest.

Continue along the tarmac drive, part of the Wealdway, for the next 1¼ miles (2km), enjoying fine views to the right across the Weald and ahead towards the wooded heights of the forest. Just after passing a row of houses on the right, turn left **B** in front of a gate along a path between wire fences, bearing right and continuing into Five Hundred Acre Wood, the 'One Hundred Acre Wood' of the *Winnie the Pooh* stories. This large area of woodland, an attractive mixture of oak, beech and conifers, was enclosed from the forest in 1693.

Cross a drive on the edge of the wood, keep ahead along another drive, bear right at a T-junction, and at a fork a little way ahead, continue along the right-hand track. At a junction of three tracks take the right-hand one (still following the Wealdway) which curves right and heads downhill following the inside edge of the

wood. Bear right at the bottom and continue gently uphill to a fork. Here the Wealdway continues to the left but you keep ahead along the right-hand track, still by the edge of Five Hundred Acre Wood, a most attractive part of the walk. Eventually, the track heads uphill between embankments to a road **C**.

At this point there has been a path diversion. Turn left along the road and at a footpath diversion sign and public footpath stone turn right over a stile. Keep ahead to cross a riding track, go through a gate and walk across a paddock. Go through another gate on the far side to cross the riding track again. Just ahead is

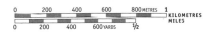

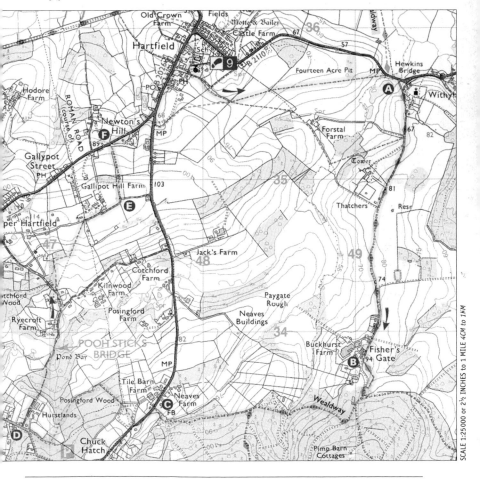

a stile and another footpath diversion sign. Climb the stile onto a track at a bend, go over another stile opposite and turn right along the edge of a field.

Follow the field edge around to the left and keep ahead to climb a waymarked stile into Posingford Wood. Continue through the wood, climb a stile on the edge of the trees and bear left. Walk across a field and climb another stile, at a public footpath stone, to re-enter woodland.

A few yards ahead the path meets a track: turn right along it and continue through a beautiful stretch of woodland to join a lane at a bend. Keep along this lane for about 100 yds (91m) and, at a sign for Pooh Bridge and a public bridleway stone, turn right **D** along a path between a fence on the left and trees on the right.

The path heads downhill along the edge of woodland to Pooh Bridge where in A.A. Milne's stories, Winnie the Pooh and his friends played 'Pooh-sticks', dropping sticks into the stream and watching them float under the bridge.

Cross the bridge and continue uphill to join a tarmac drive. Keep ahead and at a public footpath stone turn right over a stile. Walk along the left-hand edge of a field, by a hedge on the left, and follow the field-edge round to the right to climb another stile. Continue in the same direction diagonally across the next field, climbing a stile in front of a house. Bear right over the next stile, at a public footpath stone, and bear left to keep along the left-hand edge of a field.

At the end of the field climb a stile, turn left **E** to climb another one in the field corner and follow the path ahead across rough grassland, keeping parallel to the edge of woodland on the left. Go through the gate and continue – ahead is a grand view over the Medway valley and the Weald, with the spire of Hartfield church prominent – eventually going through a gate on to a road **F**.

Turn right and after ¼ mile (400m) bear left at a junction into Hartfield. ●

Pooh Bridge in Ashdown Forest

Midhurst and Cowdray Park

Start	Midhurst
Distance	6½ miles (10.5km)
Approximate time	3 hours
Parking	Midhurst – car park on North Street
Refreshments	Pubs and cafés in Midhurst
Ordnance Survey maps	Landranger 197 (Chichester & The Downs), Explorer 133 (Haslemere & Petersfield)

Midhurst is an attractive country town with a wealth of ancient buildings. Although only the earthen mound of its castle remains, the walls of Cowdray are still standing. Cowdray was one of the great palaces of Tudor England, built by the Earl of Southampton in the early 16th century; a fire in 1793 left it uninhabitable. There are fine views of its romantic ruins at the beginning and end of this walk, which also passes through lovely woodland. Cowdray Park, with its golf-course, polo-field and gallops provides an interesting final section.

Take the path from the bottom left-hand corner of the car park, which leads to Cowdray. Do not cross the bridge to the ruins but turn right and walk along the western bank of the River Rother, following its meanders until you reach the earthen ramparts of Midhurst Castle. Continue on the riverside path, which ends at a small industrial estate with a pumping station on the left **Ⓐ**. Keep straight on to cross an ancient bridge.

After the bridge turn right onto the footpath and cross a stile onto a pleasant field-edge path with woods to the right. A stile takes the path behind farm buildings to a road. Bear left and descend to a road junction where a bridleway (to Heyshott and Grafham) begins on the opposite side of the T-junction.

Turn left off the main track when this divides **Ⓑ** and climb steeply up the hill. The antiquity of this track is soon apparent: it is deeply cut into the hillside

with overhanging trees. You may well catch sight of deer. After the initial steep climb the track follows an up-and-down course. Carry straight on when another bridleway joins from the left (not shown on the map). The track soon becomes more level and sandy as it passes a plantation of conifers and crosses the aptly named Todham Rough. Turn left where the track meets another bridleway at a T-junction **Ⓒ** to enter woodland again, and then right at the junction which shortly follows.

The way now goes through chestnut woods, sheltering an abundance of game-birds. Keep straight on when a bridleway joins from the right and immediately afterwards **Ⓓ** swing left to follow the edge of the woods to a cottage. From here the track is surfaced and it soon meets Selham Road.

Turn left onto the narrow lane and after ¼ mile (400m), by a skeletal oak, turn

right onto a field-edge footpath. There is a
television mast on the skyline ahead as
the path drops towards the River Rother.
Walk on the right side of the field until
confronted with undergrowth ahead,
and then cross to the field on the right,
following its edge for a few yards to find a
signpost. Bear right here, still following
the edge of the field, with the river below
to the left beyond nettlebeds. At the end
of the field a stile takes the path to the
riverside. Follow the river to reach the
road at Ambersham Bridge.

Cross the bridge and follow the lane,
crossing straight over when it meets with
the main Petworth to Midhurst road
(A272) to a sunken path opposite **E**. An
enjoyable short stretch climbing through
woods ends where the path meets a lane
at the top. Turn right and then after
walking 100 yds (91m) turn left onto a
bridleway along the western side of
Heathend Copse. Note that the right-of-
way lies inside the wood and is not the
track on the edge of the field. Here too
there are large flocks of tame pheasants.

Just before the end of the copse a
footpath leaves to the left **F**. Take this to
cross to the plantation opposite and then
turn left onto the path along its edge. At
the end of the copse the right-of-way
strikes south-west across Cowdray Park.
The tiny Steward's Pond soon comes into
view, and the path skirts the southern
edge of this before it crosses a pony-track
and climbs a declivity on the edge of the
golf-course. Near the top of this little
valley, in a clump of trees **G**, bear left to
cross a fairway to a shelter opposite. Now
head downhill, with a fairway to the left,
keeping to the rough ground. Make for an
enormous oak tree and watch out for golf
balls in flight. From the large oak you will
see a group of trees further on and a signpost to the road. When you get to the
road, turn right and walk along it to the
top of the hill where a kissing-gate on the
left **H** gives access to a field.

Walk diagonally across the field
making for the right of the town –
Cowdray is clearly visible from here. A
signpost and a stile come into view; after
the latter, descend to another stile by a
group of trees, and at the end of a bottle-
necked meadow turn right. In the paddock
which follows, the path keeps close to the
top fence to reach another stile. Climb this
and turn left onto the track which runs
from Easebourne into Midhurst. When
you come to the ruins of Cowdray (which
are open to the public on most afternoons
in the summer), turn right and cross the
bridge onto a path which leads back to the
starting point. ●

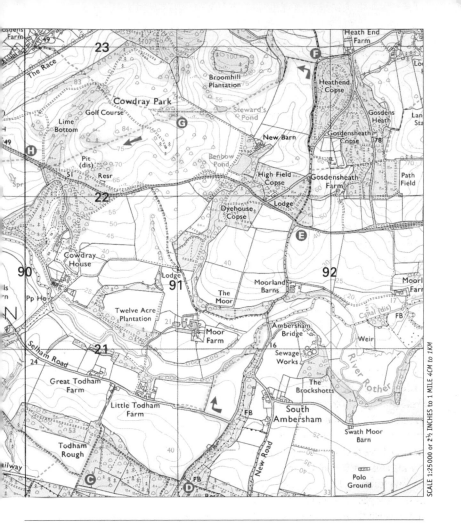

SCALE 1:25000 or 2½ INCHES to 1 MILE 4CM to 1KM

Cowdray, said to have been burnt down because of a curse on the Browne family who owned it

Hastings Country Park

Start	Hastings Old Town
Distance	5 miles (8km)
Approximate time	2½ hours
Parking	Hastings
Refreshments	Pubs and cafés at Hastings
Ordnance Survey maps	Landranger 199 (Eastbourne & Hastings), Explorer 124 (Hastings & Bexhill)

Hastings Country Park encompasses the spectacular stretch of coast that lies immediately to the east of the town. After climbing the East Cliff, you follow a roller-coaster route along the sandstone cliffs for nearly 2 miles (3.2km) before turning inland and continuing through attractive wooded glens, rejoining the cliffs to return to Hastings. Although a fairly short walk, it contains several stiff climbs.

Hastings first became a popular seaside resort in the early 19th century, and some elegant Regency architecture survives from this period. At the eastern end of the seafront, however, is the Old Town: the site of an ancient fishing settlement, one of the original Cinque Ports and a thriving community until a combination of French raids and severe storms destroyed its medieval prosperity. The Old Town's attractive narrow streets, tile-hung houses, old fishermen's cottages and medieval churches lie sandwiched between the West and East Cliffs. On West Cliff stand the meagre ruins of Hastings Castle, one of the earliest castles in the country, begun by William the Conqueror while he was waiting to fight Harold for the throne of England in that fateful month of October 1066. Despite its name, the battle was not fought at Hastings but about 7 miles (11.3km) to the north, where the town of Battle now stands.

The walk starts in the Old Town near the tourist information centre at the bottom of East Cliff. With your back to the sea turn right, towards the unique 'Net Shops' – the tall, fishermen's huts still used for drying nets – and then turn left to climb Tamarisk Steps. After the first flight turn left along a street and then turn right up a second flight to reach the top of East Cliff, to the left of the cliff railway station. Alternatively, the railway can be used.

You now enter Hastings Country Park, where a series of short, numbered posts makes route-finding easy. Starting at the first of these, inscribed 'Cliff Walks and Glens', walk along the edge of the smooth, grassy clifftop, with lovely views ahead across the crumbly sandstone cliffs. Where the grassy expanse ends continue downhill into woodland. At a fork turn right, in the direction of Ecclesbourne Glen and Fire Hills, head steeply down steps into the wooded glen, cross a tiny stream and head equally steeply up steps on the other side. Follow the direction of a yellow waymark to the left,

SCALE 1:26316 or about 2½ INCHES to 1 MILE 3.8CM to 1KM

0	200	400	600	800 METRES	1
0	200	400	600 YARDS	½	

KILOMETRES
MILES

keep ahead at the next waymark, and at the third one turn right to head back to the edge of the cliffs. Now continue along a clifftop path which gives fine views, both along the coast and inland over a pleasant, varied and peaceful landscape of fields, farms and areas of woodland.

Descend into Fairlight Glen and at post 10 keep ahead (in the direction of Lover's Seat, Coastguard, Fire Hills) through more beautiful woodland. Ignore the yellow waymark to the right a bit further on, which only leads down to the beach, and continue steeply uphill to post 11, where you bear left , in the direction of Fairlight Glen (Upper) and Barley Lane, to head inland. Follow a most attractive path along the edge of the steep-sided and thickly wooded glen, turning sharp left to a junction of paths and post 9. Bear right, following directions to Barley Lane and North Seat, along a path which emerges from the wooded glen and continues to a stile. Climb it and walk along the hedge-lined track in front which bends right to reach a tarmac track .

Turn left along this for ¼ mile (400m), go past a gate and opposite a public footpath sign to Ore and Fairlight Road turn left along a track, bearing slightly right to climb a stile. Continue along the path which heads gently downhill into woodland, curving first to the left and later to the right. At post 6 keep ahead in the direction of Ecclesbourne Glen and Hastings, and at the next fork continue along the right-hand downhill path, passing to the left of Ecclesbourne Reservoir which can just be glimpsed through the trees.

At post 5, keep ahead in the direction of Ecclesbourne Glen (Lower) and Hastings along a wide grassy path between bracken, trees and hedges to post 4, where you bear right to rejoin the outward route . Now retrace your steps down into the glen, with a steep climb up the other side and over East Hill. From here there are splendid views over Hastings Old Town, the castle on West Cliff and along the coast to the South Downs on the horizon. Finally, descend to Hastings by the steps or cliff railway. ●

Battle

Start	Battle
Distance	6 miles (9.7km)
Approximate time	3½ hours
Parking	Battle – Mount Street car park
Refreshments	Pubs and cafés at Battle
Ordnance Survey maps	Landranger 199 (Eastbourne & Hastings), Explorer 124 (Hastings & Bexhill)

This route uses a number of little-used paths and bridleways around Battle. One of them is particularly interesting – the stretch of Wadhurst Lane which retains an almost medieval character and atmosphere. Route-finding can be difficult in places and there are some overgrown and muddy sections, so follow the directions carefully, wear good boots and beware of exposing legs to thorns and nettles.

On 14 October 1066 the most famous battle in English history was fought on a hill about 7 miles (11.3km) to the north of Hastings. Before the crucial encounter William the Conqueror vowed that if God granted him victory over Harold, he would show his gratitude by building an abbey. The vow was fulfilled, Battle Abbey arose on the actual site of the battle and a town grew up around it. Today little of the church is left and some of the abbey buildings are in private hands but the 14th-century gatehouse and the monks' dormitory survive.

Begin by walking to Mount Street at the top of the car park and turn left. At the main street of Battle turn right and then right again onto the London road at the roundabout. Cross the road and after 100 yds (91m) bear left up a ramp leading to council offices picturesquely named 'The Watch Oak'. Walk through the car park and the yard which follows to a cinder track at the end. Turn right onto this and, just before 'Kelklands', branch

off it to the left onto another track running behind the bungalow. This descends to a gate and stile giving access to a meadow. Cross the field diagonally, heading for a cottage and farm on the opposite side of a small valley. There is another stile (and a bridge over a ditch) by the edge of woods at the bottom. The direction of the path is shown by a yellow waymark.

Walk up to the farm, keeping the hedge on the right. Cross the farm drive **Ⓐ** to reach a gate to the right of a cottage. A short path leads to a stile into a paddock. Continue across this to a gate on the opposite side by farm buildings. A stile on the left, by an electricity post, gives onto a vague path which skirts round the farmyard, past the back of a silage pit, to a concrete drive ending at a gate. Beyond this there is a short length of pleasant farm track, and when this ends the right-of-way continues along the right-hand edge of a field.

At the end of the field there is a stile by

an enormous uprooted tree **B**. This gives access to Wadhurst Lane, where you should turn right. Wadhurst Lane is an ancient track which sees few walkers and at this point the bridleway is overgrown by brambles and nettles. Continue in a north-easterly direction to reach a remarkable feature of the walk. The track enters a ravine etched deeply into the hard bedrock. Steps are cut into this at one point where the lane climbs steeply. It eventually emerges onto a grassy path between trees. A pond will be seen on the left. Bear right after this, continuing to follow the banks of the ancient track as it winds through the trees, but on no account cross the open ground in front of the pine forest. Open countryside is reached at last **C**, with fine views to the east, and a farm track takes the route to Netherfield Road.

Turn left, and shortly turn right at the Battle Golf Club sign. Follow the winding, metalled road beside the golf course, descending and then ascending. At the brow of the hill, pass an iron gate on the right, and immediately turn left

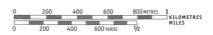

Wadhurst Lane – an ancient trackway

at a marker-post and go down the sunken track. When the path emerges from the trees and meets a crossing track **D**, turn left and almost immediately turn right onto the golf course, keeping well to the trees on the right. The path now runs in a straight line to the far right-hand corner of the course, where there is a gate by a large oak. Go through this gate onto a strange, raised track, which runs past a series of pits (lime, iron and gypsum were once produced in the area using the abundant timber); there is a bridge over a spring and a lily pond a little further on. When you reach the main London road, cross it to reach a concrete track directly opposite, signposted to Ittington Manor.

Leave the driveway to the left **E** before the manor-house, walking past a converted barn to a red gate. Go through this to a slurry tank and the skeleton of a Dutch barn. There is a bridleway junction here: keep straight on along another overgrown section to reach a gate **F**. Go through this and turn right to follow the hedgerow, heading for a white church. Pass through another gate and walk past Wood's Place. It is very easy to miss the next part of the route. By bearing to the

right you come to a derelict farmyard **G**. There is a covered strawyard on the right: the path goes through this (with the barn to the right) to reach an old stile. Climb this into a field.

Walk down the field, bearing slightly to the left with the woods to the right and the hedge close on the left. Then head for the brow of the hill, now bearing right and with the hedge to the left. You will find a bridge and stile at the bottom-left corner of the field.

Cross the next narrow field to a bridge **H** and then head directly uphill. At the top there is a stile over a fence. Go over this and you will see another stile over the fence ahead. Cross this and then climb the next field heading for the top right-hand corner, by a red house, where there is a rickety third stile among trees. Turn left after this behind a metal building. A sometimes overgrown path leads to a farm drive and this in turn leads to Whatlington Road, where you turn right towards Battle. Walk down this road for about ½ mile (800m) until you come to a road on the right and a telephone-box **J**.

Turn left here down the track known as Uckham Lane. Before the farm, turn right **K** through a green gate, and bear half right to take the path outside the hedge which bounds a caravan site to reach a stile. The path passes the left side of what appears to be a tumulus, continues to a plank bridge and emerges in a grassy field with a distant view of Battle church and the abbey gateway.

The path eventually leads past the back of allotments to a footpath junction. Go straight across here, and the footpath ends in Mount Street, in the town's main car park. ●

Bosham and Fishbourne

Start	Bosham
Distance	8½ miles (13.7km). Shorter version 5 miles (8km)
Approximate time	4½ hours (2½ hours for shorter version)
Parking	Bosham
Refreshments	Pubs and tearoom at Bosham, pubs at Fishbourne and Dell Quay
Ordnance Survey maps	Landranger 197 (Chichester & The Downs), Explorer 120 (Chichester)

The picturesque creek to the south of Bosham provides the opening section of this walk. It then strikes across country to the highest reach of Chichester harbour – an area of reedy wilderness and a sanctuary for waders and other waterbirds. The eastern shore of the estuary is equally attractive; the waterside path ends at Dell Quay. The return, which repeats a short stretch of the walk by the estuary, gives the opportunity of seeing a secluded medieval church and its neighbouring tower-house. There can be few walks which will be more enjoyable to an ornithologist. The shorter version omits the eastern shore.

Bosham, a key port in Saxon and medieval times and now a popular sailing centre, is a most attractive village with a number of historic associations. The ancient church contains the coffin of one of Canute's daughters, and it was from here that Harold, Earl of Wessex, sailed on his ill-fated trip to Normandy to his future conqueror and successor; the Bayeux Tapestry shows Harold praying in Bosham

The picturesque harbour at Bosham

church before departure.

Turn left from the car park to reach Bosham waterfront and then left again to continue along the shore of the creek. If there is a high tide you may be forced to walk on the flood wall. At the head of the creek, by a grassy triangle Ⓐ, look for a footpath sign on the other side of The Drive, to the left of a white chalet-bungalow. This is an enclosed path at the back of gardens which emerges at a road. Go straight over this onto a field path which after 1 mile (1.6km) reaches Park Lane. Turn right onto this quiet road which runs through a flat, hedgeless landscape that is reminiscent of East Anglia. At Church Farm Ⓑ bear left onto a private tarmac road, passing through a metal gate. There is a lovely distant view of Chichester Cathedral on the left. The tarmac road ends at Hook Creek Ⓒ, where the right of way is to the left, on a farm track which turns away from the estuary following a footpath sign with a curlew emblem. The track becomes a little-used footpath, and Chichester Cathedral now has a foreground of river. At a footpath junction Ⓓ turn right and walk to the river, with a hedge on the right, turning left at the tideline.

Birdlife abounds here: look out for curlews, oyster-catchers, shelducks, redshanks, red-breasted mergansers, herons, Sandwich and little terns, Brent geese, kingfishers and various migrants. The path skirts the shoreline, often on the sea wall, and is sometimes flooded briefly at high tide. Eventually the path reaches the upper end of the estuary at Fishbourne, near a thatched cottage picturesquely situated by the millpond Ⓔ.

For the shorter version of the walk, turn left onto Mill Lane here and follow route directions after Ⓔ below.

Cross over the road here (a bridleway to the 'harbour') and go through a kissing-gate, following the direction of the sign for Dell Quay. Keep bearing right through

SCALE 1:25000 or 2½ INCHES to 1 MILE 4CM to 1KM

| 0 | 200 | 400 | 600 | 800 METRES | 1 |
| 0 | 200 | 400 | 600 YARDS | ½ | KILOMETRES MILES |

the meadows, keeping as close as possible to the shoreline (though there is a short-cut across a meadow at one point on the landward side), before reaching the Crown and Anchor on Dell Quay Ⓕ.

Take the road from the pub, walking eastwards for about ½ mile (800m) before taking the left turn to Apuldram. Keep on past the drive to the Aviation Museum and Rosefield. Before the second part of a Z-bend Ⓖ turn left to pass by Rymans, an early 15th-century tower-house built by William Ryman and substantially enlarged in later centuries. The stone for the medieval house was brought from a quarry at Ventnor on the Isle of Wight,

which was also the source for the bell-tower of Chichester Cathedral. The path leads into Apuldram churchyard, where the church itself is one of the county's lesser-known gems. Its interior was comprehensively restored by a wealthy 19th-century parson who kept his steam yacht on the river nearby.

The footpath continues from the west end of the churchyard and soon reaches the waterside footpath trodden earlier. Turn right onto this and retrace your footsteps to the millpond at Fishbourne **E**. Turn right onto Mill Lane and left at the end when it reaches the main road by the Bull's Head pub.

Walk down the road towards Bosham, passing a road on the right leading to Fishbourne Roman Palace. The remains contain fine mosaics and exhibits, and a reconstruction of a Roman garden. The palace is thought to have belonged to a native British chief who co-operated with the Romans and was well rewarded for his loyalty. It was discovered by accident in 1960 by a water-board workman.

Keep on the main road to the Black Boys pub, where you fork left down Old Park Lane. Carry straight on down a private road when the lane bends left **H**. There is a footpath sign at this point. After the infilled Bullrush Pond the path continues by the side of a fine line of poplars, with a tree nursery to the right, and eventually ends when it meets a road at an acute bend. Keep straight on here and at a subsequent junction to return to Bosham.

●

The Devil's Punchbowl

Start	Hindhead
Distance	5½ miles (8.9km)
Approximate time	3 hours
Parking	National Trust car park on eastern edge of Hindhead
Refreshments	Pubs and cafés in Hindhead
Ordnance Survey maps	Landranger 186 (Aldershot & Guildford), Explorer 133 (Haslemere & Petersfield)

The Devil's Punchbowl is probably Surrey's most celebrated natural feature. This route follows its western rim before dropping down to cross to its eastern side. After climbing to the Portsmouth road, two little-used footpaths lead to Gibbet Hill – a superb viewpoint. From here it is a straightforward route back to Hindhead. There are some steep and lengthy climbs on this walk.

Beyond a gate, a roughly surfaced track leads northwards from the western end of the National Trust car park. After about 300 yds (273m), bear left at a 'tree stump' post with waymarks on top. Breaks in the trees start to occur more frequently, allowing spectacular views to the bottom of the natural amphitheatre. There is also a thoughtfully placed seat where you can sit and enjoy the scene.

By an electricity substation which has a tall mast nearby **A**, fork slightly right and in 40 yds (36m) pass under a tall green metal barrier, heading for Highcombe Copse on a broad sandy track along the western edge of the Punchbowl.

Here there is open woodland with a frequent thick understorey of bracken. Occasional views show the ground falling away dramatically to your right. After 500 yds (455m), at a low wooden post, where the track forks three ways, take the furthest right fork **B** on a path which is a detour to an excellent viewpoint. A memorial to the brothers of

W.A. Robertson stands here. Both were killed in the First World War, and the Devil's Punchbowl was given to the National Trust by the Robertson family to commemorate the men's sacrifice.

Continue past the monument to return to the main path which descends gently to reach a point where a footpath leaves to the left. Keep straight on, both here and further on when another bridleway comes in from the right. Make sure that you still have the power line in sight on the left, as the path will now begin to descend more steeply through Vanhurst Copse and in doing so becomes narrow and enclosed. A National Trust boundary-marker shows where you leave Trust land.

The steep path can be heavy-going after wet weather, but eventually it reaches Hyde Lane. Turn right here **C** to pass Ridgeway Farm. Now there is another steep section down a path with high banks to a footbridge over a small stream **D**.

Bear right after this up a track, forking left to reach a lane. Turn left again and then right **E** after 100 yds (91m), following the red arrow waymark of the Greensand Way. A long climb up a shady track with a good surface brings you to a National Trust signboard where the track divides. Bear right here, continuing to follow the Greensand Way, and then left a little further on. Go straight over the footpath junction which follows almost immediately. The climb continues, but at last the scenery changes to heathland and the sandy path reaches the top of the ridge, where there are views and a seat which overlooks the Punchbowl.

The sound of traffic on the Portsmouth road is now impossible to ignore – before reaching it there is a diversionary path to the left which avoids the churned bridleway and allows better views of the Punchbowl.

Cross the road **F** to a footpath just to the left of where you emerge onto the busy highway. This is not the Greensand Way but a more obscure footpath, marked FP94. Turn sharply to the left where the path divides, away from both alternative ways, which look better used. The path descends steeply to a forest track that continues downhill. Cross a second gravelled forestry road to take a similar one heading west, which leads to Begley Farm.

Turn right here onto the road **G** and walk along it until just before Boundless Farm it swings left. Turn right at this corner **H** onto a footpath into Boundless Copse. Keep straight ahead when the path meets a forestry track and where this divides fork left. A steep climb follows through new plantings to a clearance at the top. The path is now on the crest of a

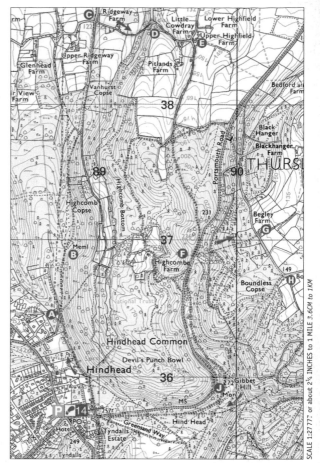

SCALE 1:27777 or about 2¼ INCHES to 1 MILE 3.6CM to 1KM

ridge and it continues to gain height as the ridge grows broader. At a footpath junction go straight across to reach Gibbet Hill **J**, with its monument and triangulation pillar. It is justly famous as a viewpoint.

With your back to the monument, walk westwards (with a small planting of trees on the right) to a car park, then continue down the road which leads from it. The Sailor's Grave is on the right, overlooking the Punchbowl. The unknown seafarer was murdered nearby in 1786. The culprits were caught and after execution their bodies were left to the mercy of the elements on the hilltop gibbet. The road from the car park leads to the main road opposite the car park where the walk started. ●

Leith Hill and Friday Street

Start	National Trust's Landslip car park below Leith Hill, near Coldharbour village
Distance	6½ miles (10.5km)
Approximate time	3½ hours
Parking	Landslip car park
Refreshments	Pub at Friday Street, kiosk at Leith Hill Tower (weekends)
Ordnance Survey maps	Landranger 187 (Dorking, Reigate & Crawley), Explorer 146 (Dorking, Box Hill & Reigate)

At 965ft (294m) Leith Hill is not only the highest point in Surrey but also the highest in south-east England. It is a magnificent viewpoint, one of a series that crown the well-wooded greensand ridge a few miles south of the North Downs. This walk is mostly through the lovely pine and beech woods and over areas of sandy heathland that is characteristic of greensand country, and although fairly hilly in places it is relatively undemanding. However, do follow the route instructions carefully; the large number of tracks and paths in this area, much of which is owned by the National Trust, can be confusing at times.

Begin by taking a path that leads up from the car park, following the first of a series of signs with a tower symbol on them, towards Leith Hill Tower. At a track turn right to head quite steeply uphill. Bear left in front of a gate marked 'Bridleway' at a junction and climb again to reach Leith Hill Tower Ⓑ. This was built in 1766 by Richard Hull of nearby Leith Hill Place to compensate for the hill just failing to top the 1000ft (305m) mark; the extra height pushes it to 1029ft (313m). There is a small admission charge to the tower, from where there is one of the finest and most extensive panoramas in the south-east: northwards across to the North Downs and beyond that to London and the Chilterns, and southwards over the Weald to the South Downs and the English Channel.

Just past the tower the path forks. Take the right-hand path here, at a second fork take the left-hand one and at a third fork take the left-hand one again. Shortly after, a well-defined path joins from the left. Continue ahead for about ½ mile (800m), following the straight main path across Wotton Common to reach a crosstrack Ⓒ. Turn right here along a fairly straight path and after ½ mile (800m) bear left at a T-junction to a lane Ⓓ. Turn left and almost immediately turn right, at a public footpath sign, along a path that keeps along the inside edge of woodland, with a fence on the right.

On the edge of the woodland go through a fence gap and follow a path across a field to climb a stile at the far end. Continue along an enclosed path to the right of houses, soon re-entering woodland, and descend, by a wire fence on the left, to a crossroads **E**. Turn right along a track that winds through the beautiful woodlands of Abinger Bottom, briefly emerging from the trees to reach a lane. Keep ahead along the lane and opposite the drive to a house called St Johns bear right to continue along a wooded track. After passing a barrier the track becomes a tarmac lane, which you follow through the charming and secluded hamlet of Friday Street to a T-junction.

Turn right to pass across the end of the millpond, a former hammer pond and one of many in the area that were created to power the hammers of the local ironworks up to the time of the Industrial Revolution. The view across it nowadays could hardly be more tranquil. On the far side, turn half-right **F**, at a public footpath sign, along a path that heads uphill away from the pond, passing to the left of a National Trust sign for Severells Copse, and continue steadily uphill to a lane. Cross over, keeping ahead to cross another lane and continue along the path in front. Take the right-hand path at a fork – not easy to spot – and head downhill along a sunken path, bearing slightly right on meeting another path to continue downhill, curving left to a lane.

SCALE 1:25000 or 2½ INCHES to 1 MILE 4CM to 1KM

Turn left through Broadmoor, another attractive and secluded hamlet, and opposite a riding centre turn sharp right , at Greensand Way and public bridleway waymarks, onto a track. Keep on this straight and broad track through Broadmoor Bottom for 1 mile (1.6km) and, just over ¼ mile (400m) after passing to the right of Warren Farm, look out for a crossing of paths and tracks by a bench **H**. Turn half-left here onto a path; after a few yards cross a stream, by a National Trust sign for Duke's Warren, and a few yards further on at a fork take the right-hand path. This is a most delightful part of the walk, initially between woodland on the right and more open sloping heathland dotted with trees on the left, later the path re-enters woodland and heads steadily uphill, finally curving left to a junction.

Bear left for a few yards to a fork and take the right-hand track, following the direction of a blue waymark, to emerge alongside the right-hand edge of the cricket pitch on Coldharbour Common. Just after the end of the cricket pitch, turn sharp right to continue along a path that has a wooden footpath post **J**, ignoring all side turns and following the main path all the while. To the left there are grand views over the Weald to the South Downs on the horizon. Opposite a barrier on the right **A**, turn left to rejoin the outward route and head downhill back to Landslip car park, following footpath signs that have a car symbol with the letter 'L' on them.

Friday Street, a delightful hamlet in the heart of rural Surrey

Albury Downs and St Martha's Hill

Start	Newlands Corner
Distance	7 miles (11.3km). Shorter version 2½ miles (4km)
Approximate time	3½ hours (1½ hours for shorter version)
Parking	Newlands Corner
Refreshments	Refreshment kiosk at Newlands Corner
Ordnance Survey maps	Landranger 186 (Aldershot & Guildford), Explorer 145 (Guildford & Farnham)

From the starting point on the Albury Downs near Guildford – part of the North Downs and one of their finest viewpoints – this walk twice descends below the crest of the downs and twice climbs to regain it. Open downland interspersed with frequent, attractive wooded stretches makes for a good, varied walk, especially when allied with superb and extensive views from the highest points at Newlands Corner and St Martha's Church. Of the two climbs the first one that ascends St Martha's Hill is quite steep and strenuous; the second that returns you to the start is more gradual. The shorter version includes only the latter.

Starting with your back to the refreshment kiosk, turn half-right, head downhill across the grass to pick up a path and bear right along it, soon passing a yellow waymarker-post with an acorn symbol on it, indicating that this is part of the North Downs Way. Now follow a splendidly scenic path, below the edge of woodland on the right and with extensive views over the downs to the left. At a fork take the left-hand path and do the same at the next fork, keeping along the right-hand edge of woodland. Soon the path enters the trees, bends to the left and heads down to a lane **A**.

Cross over, go up some steps and turn left, at a North Downs Way sign, along an enclosed, wooded path that heads downhill, parallel to the lane on the left, to a T-junction of paths in front of a house **B**.

*At this point those who wish to do the shorter version of the walk should turn left to rejoin the main route after ¼ mile (400m) at **K** below.*

Turn right here, leaving the North Downs Way, along a path that keeps by the left-hand edge of woodland; later this path broadens into a track. Climb a stile beside a metal gate and continue, passing through a farmyard to reach a lane **C**. Cross over, take the enclosed track ahead at a public bridleway sign, and at a crossing of tracks by a wooden seat, keep ahead into woodland. The track curves left to a T-junction where you turn right, rejoining the North Downs Way along a track between wire fences. Over to the right, houses on the edge of Guildford can be seen. The track keeps along the right-hand edge of Chantries Wood – along this

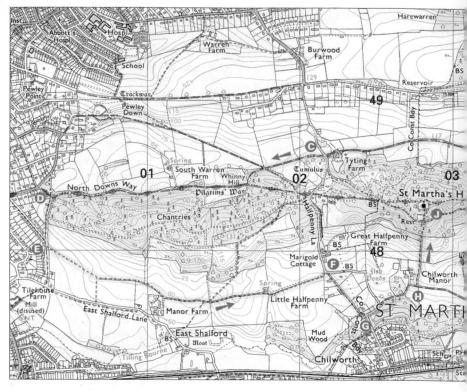

section the North Downs Way coincides with the Pilgrims' Way – finally going to the right of a cottage to a crossing of tracks **D**. Turn left along an enclosed path, still keeping along the right-hand edge of Chantries Wood, and on reaching a road bear left.

After 50 yds (45m) turn left **E** over a stile at a public footpath sign and walk across the middle of a field, later continuing by a hedge on the right. Turn right over a stile near a farm, turn left to continue in the same direction, now along an undulating track, eventually going

Newlands Corner – one of the finest viewpoints on the North Downs Way

superb viewpoint looking out over the North Downs, Guildford, along the greensand ridge and across the Weald to the distant South Downs. This isolated hilltop church (the parish church of Chilworth) was rebuilt in 1850, partly from the stones of the original Norman church that stood on the site. It is one of the major landmarks on the North Downs Way.

At the church, turn right along a broad, sandy track that heads downhill, with grand views along the greensand ridge ahead, continuing through woodland to reach a junction. Keep straight ahead, passing to the right of a ruined wartime pillbox, and at a junction of three tracks take the left-hand one that leads through a car park to a lane **K**.

Here you rejoin the shorter route. Turn right and after 50 yds (45m) bear left along a straight, fence-lined path which runs below the crest of the Albury Downs on the left, later continuing along the left-hand edge of woodland. Once more this is part of the supposed line of the Pilgrims' Way. Go through a gate at a public bridleway sign and bear slightly right across a field, making for a metal gate in the wire fence that marks the field boundary. Go through this and turn left along a path. Pass through a wooden gate and continue along a path, by woodland on the right, which heads downhill to a T-junction **L**.

Turn left, keep ahead at a fork a few yards in front and follow a sunken, enclosed track steadily uphill back to the start, first bearing right, later turning left at a T-junction of tracks, and continuing up to regain the ridge of the downs at Newlands Corner.

SCALE 1:25 000 or 2½ INCHES to 1 MILE 4CM to 1KM

through a gate onto a lane **F**. Turn right and almost immediately right again, at a public footpath sign, to continue along a hedge-enclosed path which descends to a lane **G**. Turn left here and where the lane bends sharply to the left keep ahead, at a public bridleway sign, through a white gate to the left of a lodge. Continue along a tarmac track through the grounds of Chilworth Manor.

The track curves left, keeping to the right of the manor-house. At a fork turn right and go along a rough track between fences. After 50 yds (45m) turn left **H**, at a public footpath sign, along an enclosed path which heads steeply up St Martha's Hill, the most strenuous part of the walk but leading to one of the finest views in Surrey. On the upper slopes of the hill the path re-enters woodland, crosses a sandy track and continues up to St Martha's Church **J**, 573ft (175m) high and a

Hambledon, Hascombe and the Hurtwood

Start	Hambledon
Distance	6½ miles (10.5km)
Approximate time	3 hours
Parking	Hambledon – car park at end of lane opposite churchyard (do not use church spaces on Sundays)
Refreshments	Pub at Hascombe
Ordnance Survey maps	Landranger 186 (Aldershot & Guildford), Explorers 133 (Haslemere & Petersfield), 134 (Crawley & Horsham) and 145 (Guildford & Farnham)

Most of this walk is through varied woodland. At the start there are tidy groves of coppiced chestnut, followed by older plantings and some examples of the remnants of indigenous forest. Hydon's Ball and Vann Hill are both excellent viewpoints.

From the car park at Hambledon church take the footpath that goes left past the churchyard wall (note the ancient lime-kiln on the right). Go through the gate and cross the field via a well-used path. Cross the next field diagonally, heading towards a wooded hill. On the far side of the field go through a kissing-gate and through an avenue of coppiced chestnuts. At the first junction turn left to climb Hydon's Ball **A** – a strange name for a hill.

Trees screen the magnificent view northwards until the summit is reached. The large seat here is a memorial to Octavia Hill, one of the founders of the National Trust, who donated this land in 1915. Today, the hilltop contains an underground reservoir – hence the various covers and vents which can be seen here.

Retrace route downhill to the first crossing path. Turn right, soon passing a memorial stone on the left. Continue along the path, heading downhill to reach a fence. Turn right and, keeping the fence on the left, go through the wood – the path becomes fainter. When the fence ends at a junction **B**, turn right onto a bridleway, and then, after a short distance, bear right at the next junction. This long section ends when the bridleway, having crossed one further track, meets the road.

Turn right, and after ¼ mile (400m), just as the road bends right to begin a descent down a steep hill, take the bridleway on the left **C** which heads northwards on the left side of Juniper Valley. This can be seen through a fringe of trees on the right, beyond a lovely meadow. Very soon the path swings to the left away from this and begins to descend, gently at first but then more steeply. The head of the valley will be seen to the right. Turn sharply right at the bottom **D**.

The climb up the eastern side of the valley is energetic for a few minutes, then the path drops down into Austen's Wood before climbing again with the extensive garden of High Barn to the right. A

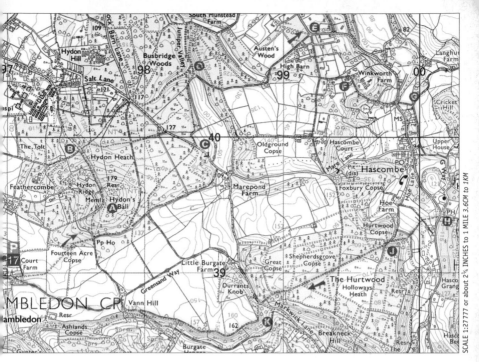

SCALE 1:27777 or about 2¼ INCHES to 1 MILE 3.6CM to 1KM

surfaced driveway takes the bridleway the last few yards to the road.

Turn sharply right here **E**, avoiding the busy road, onto the lane past Garden Cottage and High Leybourne which goes to Hascombe Court. Turn to the left well before this, however, onto the surfaced bridleway going to High Winkworth. Bear to the right before High Hascombe **F** onto a bridleway that descends steeply to the village. This bridleway joins a lane to the main road which passes picturesque Elm Cottage, then it continues on the other side of the road, past paddocks, to reach a junction **G**, where you turn right. Keep straight on after The Stables and turn right when the path meets the tarmac road leading to the pond, church and pub.

Cross the main road by the White Horse pub to a footpath **H** – part of the Greensand Way – which strikes across the meadow to a stile. Climb the edge of the next meadow to another stile at the top, which takes the path into a wood. Immediately after this stile, fork right, following the direction indicated by the waymark. A steep climb takes the path to a

bridleway. Bear right here and continue climbing. There is another track to the right just below. Turn right and then left at the end of the climb and cross straight over a track **J** into an area of scrubby heath – the Hurtwood – which suffered in the 1987 hurricane. Some pine trees, their tops snapped off, still stand as testimony to the force of the wind. The Hurtwood is a strange, claustrophobic place – high up, but without any views. The track descends to Markwick Lane.

Cross the lane to a bridleway opposite, forking left almost immediately to climb to the top of the valley **K**. Here there is a path on the edge of the meadow, with tree-tops to the left. The view to the south is soon screened by trees. Do not descend when a path joins from the left – though the main path often drops a little into the wood, it never loses much height.

Turn right onto the lane at Vann Hill and then left before Maple Bungalow onto the bridleway back to Hambledon church. ●

Ashdown Forest

Start	Gills Lap car park, at junction of B2026 (to Hartfield) and minor road to Forest Row
Distance	6½ miles (10.5km)
Approximate time	3½ hours
Parking	Gills Lap
Refreshments	None
Ordnance Survey maps	Landrangers 188 (Maidstone & The Weald of Kent) and 198 (Brighton & The Downs), Explorer 135 (Ashdown Forest)

Nowadays Ashdown Forest mainly comprises a large elevated area of open heathland, covered with gorse, bracken and heather and dotted with random pines and birches – the nearest there is to a wilderness in south-east England. It is administered by a board of conservators who allow unrestricted access and provide a whole series of parking areas along the roads that criss-cross the forest. Paradoxically, this freedom of access and consequently the large number of tracks and paths can cause route-finding problems, making it difficult to stick to a precise path. Fortunately, much of this walk keeps parallel and fairly close to roads and therefore it is not necessary to follow the exact route as you make your way between the various stands of pine that act as the main landmarks. Only on the last part of the walk, between points ❺ and ❼, are public footpaths used and here it is important to follow carefully the exact route directions. As route-finding is dependent on relatively few landmarks, it is not advisable to attempt this walk in poor visibility.

Ashdown Forest was once part of the vast ancient forest of Andredesweald that stretched from Kent right across Surrey and Sussex into Hampshire, and originally covered an area of 18,000 acres (7285 ha) between Tunbridge Wells, East Grinstead and Lewes. Like the other forests of the Weald, its woodlands were progressively felled to meet the demands of both the local iron industry and the navy and it became considerably reduced in size. At various times the forest has belonged to both royal and private landowners, and its history has been characterised by almost constant conflict between the desire of the owners to enclose it and the determination of the inhabitants to preserve their common rights. Eventually these disputes were settled by a legal decision in the 19th century, and since 1885 the remaining 6000 acres (2428 ha) of open heathland that constitute the present forest have been under the control of a board of conservators.

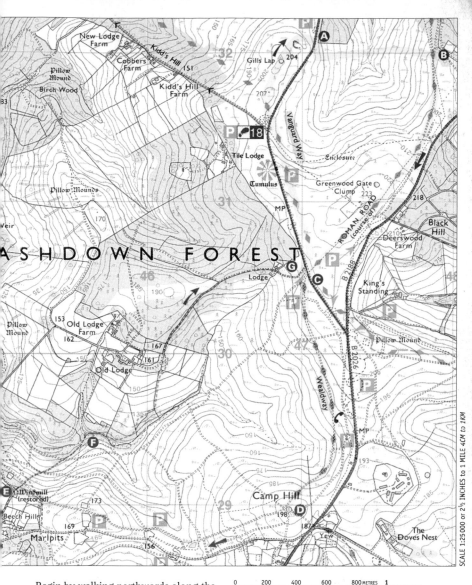

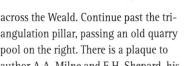

SCALE 1:25000 or 2½ INCHES to 1 MILE 4CM to 1KM

| 0 | 200 | 400 | 600 | 800 METRES | 1 |
| 0 | 200 | 400 | 600 YARDS | ½ | |

KILOMETRES
MILES

Begin by walking northwards along the broad track (almost all the tracks across the forest are broad) that runs to the left of and parallel to the road to Hartfield, to reach the triangulation pillar at Gills Lap just to the right of the track. Gills Lap Clump is one of a number of stands of tall pines dotted around this high heathland, apparently planted in the early 19th century to enhance the landscape; they are indispensable landmarks for walkers. It is one of the highest points in the forest at 671 ft (204m) and a magnificent viewpoint, especially looking northwards across the Weald. Continue past the triangulation pillar, passing an old quarry pool on the right. There is a plaque to author A.A. Milne and E.H. Shepard, his illustrator, on the left. About 100 yds (91m) further on – soon after the track starts to head downhill – turn right onto a grassy path that descends to the road at Piglet's car park **A**.

Cross over and take the narrow path opposite that bends to the right. This initially runs parallel to the road but after passing a barrier it curves left to join a track. Continue along this track: at first between trees, later heading uphill over open heathland with grand views ahead, then descending into a wooded hollow to cross a small stream and heading up again more steeply, keeping more or less in a straight line all the time. Cross a track, continue uphill along the path ahead and at the top turn right along a second track **B** (a few yards to the right of a fork), here joining the Wealdway. Follow this track and the various Wealdway markers – short posts with 'W/W' on them – passing to the left of Greenwood Gate Clump. This is another stand of pines, a superb viewpoint and, at 732ft (223m), the highest point in Ashdown Forest. Keep parallel to the B2188 on the left – unseen for the most part if not unheard. Although the proliferation of tracks and paths on this section of the walk is confusing, keep in a roughly straight line to emerge at the B2026 **C**.

Cross the road to the left of the car park and – continuing on the Wealdway – take the first fork to the left. The track bears gradually left to keep parallel with the B2026 on the left and heads up to the prominent circle of pines and the triangulation pillar at Camp Hill **D**, 650ft (198m) high – another magnificent viewpoint over the forest. Continue past the trees, bearing right and still keeping along the track, parallel with the road on the left. Pass through Ellison's Pond car park, keep ahead to pass through another, continue uphill over a small rise, known as Friends Clump, and then descend gently along a grassy track. Where you see the sign 'Windmill', bear left off the track along a parallel path, go through a gate and Nutley Windmill is just ahead **E**. If you happen to take one of the several alternative parallel routes you can hardly fail to arrive at the windmill, a prominent landmark and the oldest working windmill in Sussex.

At the windmill, turn right over a way-marked stile and at a fork ahead, take the right-hand path through bracken and trees, heading down to rejoin the grassy track that you were previously on. Turn right along it for about 50 yds (45m) and then turn left to continue downhill along a clear and wide track, bearing slightly right. It is important to get onto the correct path here. This narrow but clear path initially keeps parallel with the track, along the right-hand edge of woodland and soon enters the trees to reach a fork. Here take the left-hand, lower path that leads more deeply into the wood, by a stream on the left. Go through gateposts and keep straight on to a waymarked footbridge over the stream a few yards ahead. Turn right **F** to cross the stream and follow the directions of a fingerpost and waymark on the right to walk along a narrow, uphill path between trees and bushes. Following the way-marks, bear to the right along a broader track over a plank bridge, then keeping in a straight line until a waymark on a tall pine tree is reached. Turn left, following the footpath with trees on your right and cross two stiles with a plank bridge between them. Turn left and, keeping the hedge on your left, climb gently uphill through two fields to a stile in the hedge on the left. Go over the stile onto the drive to Old Lodge – a large, rambling stone mansion. Turn right and continue gently uphill on this winding tarmac drive for just over $^3/_4$ mile (1.2km), enjoying more grand views over open expanses of forest, finally going through a metal gate between stone gateposts and continuing up to rejoin the B2026 **G**. Cross over, take the path ahead across grass and on joining a broad track – part of the Vanguard Way – turn left and follow it, keeping parallel to the road on the left and then bearing left off the Vanguard Way back to the car park at Gills Lap. ●

Arundel Park and South Stoke

Start	Arundel
Distance	7 miles (11.3km)
Approximate time	3½ hours
Parking	Mill Road car park
Refreshments	Pubs and cafés at Arundel, pub at Offham
Ordnance Survey maps	Landranger 197 (Chichester & The Downs), Explorer 121 (Arundel & Pulborough)

This lovely walk begins under the walls of Arundel Castle and then passes through the impressive park which surrounds the castle, the home of the dukes of Norfolk for 500 years. The return part of the route follows the course of the River Arun eastwards and southwards, at first through rich woodland high on a cliff overlooking the valley and then on the banks of the river itself.
Note that dogs are restricted to public rights-of-way in Arundel Park.

Castle, church and Catholic cathedral perched above a bend in the river give Arundel a continental air. The juxtaposition of the buildings reflects the uneasy relationship that existed from the Reformation to the present century between the mainly Protestant townspeople and the Catholic dukes of Norfolk, owners of the castle and premier peers of the realm.

The extensive walls and towers of Arundel Castle make a splendid sight. It is mainly a 19th-century reconstruction of the original Norman castle but some earlier work remains, including the 11th-century shell keep. Close by is the medieval church, unique in that the nave is Anglican and the east end Catholic. For a long time the two parts were walled off from each other but now they are separated by a glass screen that can be

opened on ecumenical occasions. The cathedral, an imposing building in the French Gothic style, was erected by a duke of Norfolk in the late 19th century only after the Catholic Church in England was allowed to organise itself into dioceses.

From the car park, turn left and then right when you reach the High Street. The tourist information centre is on the left side of the High Street, which climbs steeply past the medieval parish church on the right and the Catholic cathedral on the left. Opposite a primary school on the left, bear right to enter Arundel Park **Ⓐ**.

Follow the driveway into the park through a kissing-gate by a road gate. Bear right at a notice 'No unauthorised vehicles beyond this point' onto a track and continue, with the Hiorne Tower –

built by Francis Hiorne in 1790 – to your left. Cross the end of the gallop (look out for racehorses here), then turn left **B**. On your left can be seen some of the extensive re-afforestaton that has been carried out following the devastation of the 1987 storm. Continue along the track skirting a wood on the right to a field gate and stile. The track then begins a descent into a steep-sided dry valley. This part of the walk is a delight with a wide view of the park to the right and woods to the left.

At the bottom of the valley, at a three-way footpath sign, cross over to a track that climbs, via a gate in a fence, steeply heading towards Duke's Plantation, not immediately visible on the skyline. After $^1/_4$ mile (400m) on this track, swing left **C** up the slope of the valley, heading north

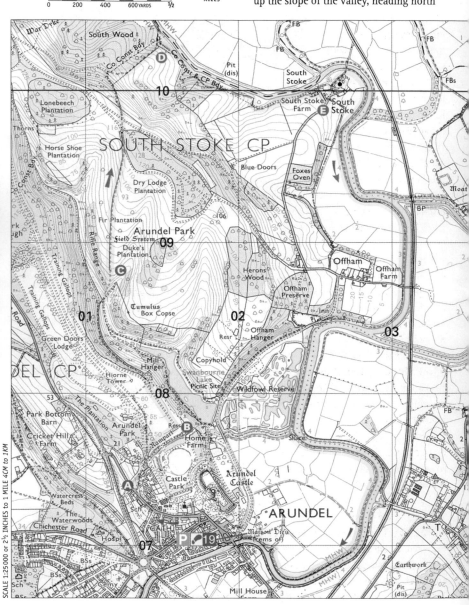

to climb to the crest of the ridge. Head for the left-hand edge of Dry Lodge Plantation.

Walk along the track here, enjoying the fine view on the left towards Duchess Lodge; behind is another splendid panorama – on a clear day you can see the Isle of Wight beyond Chichester harbour. The view ahead opens up at the top of the plantation, where a finger-post points the direction of the footpath as it leaves the track, turning half-right to head for a distant chalky cliff. You soon come to a stile by a gate, which is another excellent vantage-point for vistas over the Arun valley. Follow the track down and turn right when this meets another track at the bottom.

The Arun valley from the north edge of Arundel Park

Turn left immediately before the next gateway to leave the track and follow a faint path down by a fence, which leads into dense woodland. This becomes steep and dark and there is an old flint wall on the right. Go through a gap in this at the bottom to reach the bridleway ⒟ which follows the south bank of the River Arun. Take a few steps to the left to view the river or turn sharp right to begin the return leg of the walk.

The bridleway twists its way through woodland which screens views of the river, and eventually it leaves the wood through a gateway to reach the top of a cliff. Another climb follows, and the track becomes a field-edge path leading into South Stoke. Turn right to pass behind a cart shed, which used to have accommodation for labourers on its upper floor, and reach the lane ⒠ into the hamlet. Turn left here to visit the unpretentious and utterly peaceful little St Lawrence Church, its interior dominated by an enormous cast-iron stove. It is usually open. Continue down the lane to the bridge and turn right along the path on the west bank of the river.

The walking now is undemanding, the tranquillity disturbed only by the passing of a train or, rarely, a boat. You may see herons here and some less common waterbirds. Burpham church can be seen nestling among trees as a navigational cut truncates the eastern meander of the river. The dramatic silhouette of Arundel Castle appears as the footpath approaches a cattle bridge across the river at Offham Farm, but the apparent distance to Arundel is deceptive since the river makes another meander eastwards before reaching the town. Before this final section the river-side path passes a pub. The path ends back at Mill Road car park. ●

Wisborough Green, Arun valley and the Mens

Start	Wisborough Green
Distance	9½ miles (15.3km). Shorter version 4 miles (6.4km)
Approximate time	5 hours (2 hours for shorter version)
Parking	Around the green at Wisborough Green
Refreshments	Pubs at Wisborough Green
Ordnance Survey maps	Landranger 197 (Chichester & The Downs), Explorer 134 (Crawley & Horsham)

*From the delightful village green at Wisborough Green the route
heads across fields to the now disused Arun Canal, crosses flat
meadowland, keeping alongside the canal bank and with the
meandering River Arun for company, and then continues through
splendid woodland, a survival of the old and once extensive
forests of the Weald, before rejoining the river and returning to
Wisborough Green. Although lengthy, this is an easy walk in flat
country that has a remote feel about it, with wide vistas across a
typical Wealden landscape. Waymarking is good throughout but
some overgrown and muddy sections are likely, the former by the
disused canal and the latter on some woodland stretches. The
shorter version of the walk omits the woodland.*

It would be difficult to find a more
attractive starting point for a walk than
the spacious, tree-lined green at
Wisborough Green, large enough to stage
village cricket matches and surrounded by
fine old houses. The nearby church stands
on a low ridge above the flat countryside
of the Weald, dominated by its tower and
tall 13th-century broach-spire. It dates
from the 12th century and much Norman
work remains at the west end; inside there
is a rare 12th-century mural, discovered
during restoration work in 1867.

Start on the south side of the green
and walk along the main road in the
Billingshurst direction, passing in front of
the Three Crowns and continuing along a
paved footpath that leads directly to the
church. Go through a metal gate into the
churchyard, walk along its left-hand edge
and at the far end turn left over a stile.
Immediately turn right, continue along
the right-hand edge of two fields, by a
hedge on the right, and at the end of the
second field climb a stile to a crossing of
paths. Keep ahead to climb another stile
and walk along the edge of the next
narrow field, bearing left to a stile. Climb
it and continue along the left-hand edge
of a succession of fields and over several
stiles, eventually turning left to keep
along the left-hand edge of two more
fields and following the direction of a
footpath sign around the edge of the

second field; the path curves to the right, and finally left and right to a stile in the field corner.

Climb the stile, turn left along the main road – take care, for it is busy and there are no verges – for ¹/₄ mile (400m) and at a public footpath sign turn right over a stile . Walk along the left-hand edge of the field, by a hedge on the left, and in the field corner go through a gate, cross a footbridge over the disused Arun Canal and turn right, at a public footpath sign, alongside it Ⓑ. The canal was built between the rivers Wey and Arun to provide a link between London and the south coast. Opened in 1816 it was never a commercial success and was abandoned in 1871. The canal is being restored gradually, and most notably at Lording's Lock where the Orfold Aqueduct is being excavated.

Waterlilies on the pond at Wisborough Green

Follow a sometimes narrow and overgrown but well-waymarked path (part of the Wey-South Path) along the left-hand side of the disused canal across rough meadowland, between the canal on the right and the meandering River Arun on the left, climbing a series of stiles. There are expansive views across the Weald. At one stage you cross the River Arun above a weir, but keep to the left of the disused canal all the time until a public footpath sign directs you to the right, to cross a footbridge over it. A few yards after this, turn left to continue along the right-hand side of the canal. Approaching the river again, bear slightly left to go through a metal gate and on through a wooded area. After walking along a raised embankment, between the canal on the left and river on the right, you reach a junction of paths and footpath sign Ⓒ.

Those wishing to do the shorter version of the walk only, turn right here along a bridleway, head down to cross a footbridge over the river, keep along the left-hand edge of a field, go through a gate and continue along a track to a public bridleway sign, where you keep straight on to rejoin the main route at Ⓚ.

Keep ahead through a metal gate, once more squeezing between canal and river, and continue along the right-hand side of the canal. Where the path meets the meandering Arun again there are two footbridges ahead, one over each waterway. Turn left to cross the canal bridge, go through a metal gate and keep ahead diagonally across a field to a stile. Climb it, bear right along a track that keeps along the right-hand edge of a field, by a hedge on the right, and follow the field edge as it curves to the left, joining the left-hand side of the canal again, to reach a public bridleway sign. Here turn right through a metal gate, cross the canal for the last time, keep ahead over the river and walk across a meadow, going through two gates in quick succession.

Now keep ahead across a field to a public footpath sign and turn right along the left-hand edge of the field towards a house. Go through a gate, cross a tarmac drive and continue along a grassy path, passing to the right of the house, to another gate. Go through that, keep ahead across a narrow meadow, by a hedge on the left, go through another gate and continue along a tree-lined path, finally passing through a gate onto a lane.

Turn left, ignore the first footpath sign to the right but at the second one turn right **D** through a fence gap and continue along a path. Climb a stile to enter woodland. The next part of the walk goes through a delightful area of unspoilt woodland, characterised by tall, slender beeches – a splendid reminder of the ancient forests that once covered much of the Weald. At a fork take the right-hand path, keep ahead at a crossing of paths at a footpath sign, bear left on emerging into a small open area and pass between a cottage on the right and a duck pond on the left to reach another public footpath sign. Turn right and continue between a hedge on the right and wire fence on the left, and the path soon bears right again to re-enter the trees. Descend into a valley, cross a stream at the bottom, head up again and go through a gate and keep ahead across a narrow, grassy area, once more entering woodland, the Mens.

At the first crossing of paths and footpath sign keep ahead, but at the second crossing turn right **E** to follow a winding and undulating wooded path. On joining a tarmac track, keep along it, following public bridleway signs between the buildings of Hawkhurst Court, now a school, and after passing the buildings continue along the broad, straight tarmac drive. At a junction of several drives **F**, bear left for a few yards and then turn right along the drive to Crimbourne Stud and Barn. Just in front of gates a public footpath sign directs you to bear left onto a path; follow it through another

superb part of the Mens. On reaching a track, turn right **G**, passing to the left of a house, keep ahead along what has now become a narrow path and follow it through the woodland. After crossing a footbridge, turn right, passing a footpath sign, and continue along to a lane **H**.

Turn left, then left again at a T-junction, in the direction of Wisborough Green, and after ¼ mile (400m) turn right **J**, at a public bridleway sign, along a straight track. At the next footpath sign turn left along a hedge-lined track, look out for a public bridleway sign which directs you to the right, go through a metal gate and walk along the right-hand edge of a field, by a hedge on the right. Go through another metal gate, continue along a hedge-lined path, at the end of it bear left through a gate and keep by the right-hand edge of a field. Pass through a hedge gap to a public bridleway sign and continue

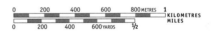

by the right-hand edge of the next field to a gate. Go through, keep along the right-hand edge of several fields – the River Arun can be seen winding below on the right – and continue along a track between fields to a T-junction, turning left **K** along another track.

Go through a metal gate into a farmyard and follow the main track as it curves first left then right to pass to the left of the farmhouse. Continue along an attractive, tree-lined tarmac track, with the church spire and houses of Wisborough Green visible ahead, back to the village. At the road, turn left to return to the village green.

Alfriston, Long Man of Wilmington and Jevington

Start	Alfriston
Distance	8 miles (12.9km)
Approximate time	4 hours
Parking	Alfriston
Refreshments	Pubs and cafés at Alfriston, pub and café at Jevington
Ordnance Survey maps	Landranger 199 (Eastbourne & Hastings), Explorer 123 (South Downs Way – Newhaven to Eastbourne)

An ancient, mysterious chalk figure and four highly attractive and distinctive villages, all with fine medieval churches, are linked by this energetic walk on the South Downs that starts and finishes in the beautiful Cuckmere valley. It combines the best of downland scenery with considerable historic appeal and offers many grand and extensive views across open, rolling country. There is plenty of climbing but nothing steep or strenuous.

A number of factors combine to make Alfriston one of the most appealing villages in Sussex. It is attractively situated below the downs on the west bank of the lovely River Cuckmere, and from the old market cross its narrow main street slopes gently downhill, lined with old houses, shops, tearooms and medieval inns. Across a charming open grassy area called the Tye stands the unusually imposing and sturdy-looking cruciform church, the 'Cathedral of the Downs', overlooking riverside meadows. Beside the church is the thatched, timber-framed, 14th-century Clergy House, which was the first building acquired by the National Trust, in 1896. Until the 18th century Alfriston was a port, and its comparative isolation near a lonely stretch of coast made it an ideal smuggling centre.

The walk begins at the market cross in the village centre. Walk down the main

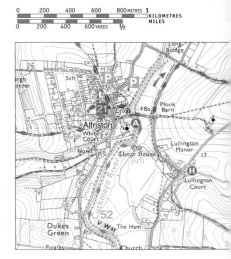

street, turn left along a tarmac path beside the United Reformed Church – there are footpath signs to Alfriston church, Clergy House and Lullington church – and after passing the church bear slightly left to continue between walls. To the right across the Tye are the medieval church and Clergy House. Keep ahead to cross a footbridge over the River Cuckmere, turn left **Ⓐ**, climb a stile and continue along a raised embankment above low-lying meadowland, parallel to the river.

Climb a stile to the right of a brick bridge, turn right along a lane to a T-junction and continue along a track, following a bridleway sign to Jevington. After passing the entrance to a house the track narrows to a sunken hedge- and tree-lined path that heads uphill and bears left to a lane **Ⓑ**. Cross over, continue along the track ahead, go through a gate and follow the track uphill onto open downland. Soon there are fine views to the coast. Pass right of a reservoir and aerial. Go through another gate and continue, bearing right to a junction of tracks.

Here turn sharp left, almost doubling back, and head downhill with a wire fence

and tumulus on the right. After 100 yds (91m) turn right through a gate and walk along a path, by a wire fence on the left, that heads across the slopes of Windover Hill to pass below the Long Man of Wilmington. In front of the chalk figure bear left to a gate and information board. The Long Man, 230ft (70m) long and cut from the chalk downland, is claimed to be the largest representation of the human figure in western Europe. His origins are obscure: he could be prehistoric, Saxon or medieval and many theories abound. The first drawings of him come from an 18th-century manuscript where the two staffs that he is holding are shown as a rake and scythe, which suggests that he was perhaps an agricultural fertility figure.

Go through the gate and follow the path ahead gently downhill, going through another gate onto a lane. Turn right to Wilmington Priory – there is a parallel footpath on the right which

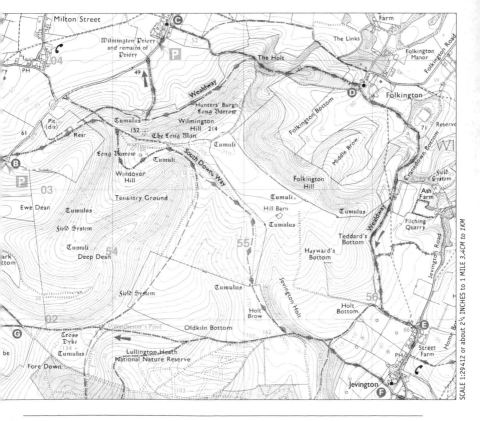

SCALE 1:29,412 or about 2¼ INCHES to 1 MILE 3.4CM to 1KM

The impressive chalk figure of the Long Man of Wilmington

rejoins the lane opposite the priory and Long Man car park. The small 12th-century church next to the priory was a dual-purpose building, serving the needs of both the local people and the monks of the priory; there were so few monks that a separate church was considered unnecessary. Although the church is predominantly Norman, the nave was rebuilt in the 14th century, and the whole building was extensively restored by the Victorians. At the west end is the usual belfry and short spire commonly found in Sussex. Note the giant ancient yew in the churchyard. Wilmington Priory is now a museum.

Opposite the church turn right **C**, at a public bridleway sign to Folkington, along a partially tree- and hedge-lined track that winds uphill, eventually entering woodland. Bear left on joining another track and continue through the attractive woodland. Later the track narrows to a path and keeps along the edge of the trees, giving excellent views to the left across the Weald, eventually heading gently downhill to a T-junction **D**. In front is Folkington's tiny, simple church.

At the T-junction, bear right along a downhill, tree-lined track and continue along an enclosed path that heads steadily uphill, curving gradually to the right and later straightens out and continues gently downhill. After 1¼ miles (2km) at a T-junction, turn left along the track into Jevington. Turn right **E** along the road through the village and, where it bears

slightly left to head downhill, continue along a path that leads into the churchyard. The church is a delightful building in a lovely spot overlooking the downs. Its west tower is Saxon, and during restoration work in 1875 a Saxon sculpture was discovered in the building.

Walk past the church and turn right **F** at a bridleway sign to Alfriston and a South Downs Way acorn symbol, along a hedge-lined path that heads gently uphill and continues along the right, inside edge of woodland. Keep ahead at a South Downs Way sign and about 50 yds (45m) further on bear left on joining a track. Continue steadily uphill through woodland and on emerging from the trees you reach a bridleway post. Here the South Downs Way turns right but you keep straight ahead.

Now there is a splendid stretch of walking along a fairly straight, undulating track across open, breezy downland, with extensive views over the downs and the thick, dark woodlands of Friston Forest to the left, passing Lullington Heath National Nature Reserve, an area of conserved chalk down. Keep straight on at a waymark in the Litlington direction, at the next bridleway sign keep ahead, but where the track forks at the next sign take the right-hand track **G** towards Lullington Court.

As you head downhill there is a fine view of Alfriston in front. The track becomes hedge-lined and eventually curves slightly right to reach a road. Turn right, take the first turning on the left **H**, signposted to Alfriston, and where the road bears slightly right keep ahead over a stile at a South Downs Way acorn symbol.

Walk along the right-hand edge of a meadow, by a hedge on the right; from here there is a lovely view across the meadow and river to Alfriston church and the Clergy House. Climb a stile and continue along a hedge-enclosed path to a T-junction. Turn left onto a tarmac path and cross the Cuckmere into Alfriston. ●

Box Hill, Ranmore Common, Norbury Park and Juniper Bottom

Start	National Trust Information Centre, Box Hill
Distance	11 miles (17.7km)
Approximate time	5 hours
Parking	National Trust car park, Box Hill
Refreshments	Take-away at start, pub at Mickleham
Ordnance Survey maps	Landranger 187 (Dorking, Reigate & Crawley), Explorer 146 (Dorking, Box Hill & Reigate)

The greater part of this route is through woodland that is recovering well from the hurricane of 1987. It is advisable to pack a picnic and to take mud-proof footwear, unless the weather has been unusually dry. In the final section of the walk, after Mickleham, there are some quite demanding climbs.

Walk past the front of the National Trust Information Centre at Fort Cottages, which take their name from a stronghold and ammunition store built here in the late 19th century, to the viewpoint and triangulation pillar **Ⓐ**. The view southwards is spectacular, with the ground dropping away almost sheer to the River Mole some 400ft (122m) below. Descend to the right of the viewpoint and turn right onto the footpath (the North Downs Way) which drops down towards Dorking.

At a waymark with a red arrow turn left to go steeply downhill through a group of yews. Steps have been cut into this path. Soon the River Mole can be glimpsed below, and you will see a signpost giving the choice of crossing the river either by stepping-stones **Ⓑ** or footbridge. The former method, bearing left, is more fun and offers the shorter route. Go up the track on the other side to the main road – the path from the footbridge rejoins here.

Take great care in crossing the dual carriageway. There is a track almost directly opposite which passes below the railway and then into the Denbies Wine estate. This vineyard covers much of the side of the valley to the east of Ranmore.

Several footpaths cross the track, but keep on the North Downs Way as it curves south for about 200 yds (183m), then at a signposted crossing of tracks **Ⓒ** turn right along a bridleway off the North Downs Way into Ashcombe Wood. After another 200 yds (183m) uphill, a footpath sign directs you to the left and further uphill. The path continues through woods, latter flattens out and becomes a metalled, then concrete road passing Denbies Farm. There may be deer in enclosures on your left. Pass straight on through a gateway to the public highway.

Carry straight on along the quiet lane to reach Ranmore. A bridleway runs along the wide verge, where walking is easier than on tarmac. Pass the Victorian flint church at Ranmore, bear right at the main road – the bridleway is now on the right – and pass the National Trust car park on the left. Immediately after the three houses on the right (the third, called Fox Cottages, has pantiles and tall chimneys) there is a track with a sign to the youth hostel 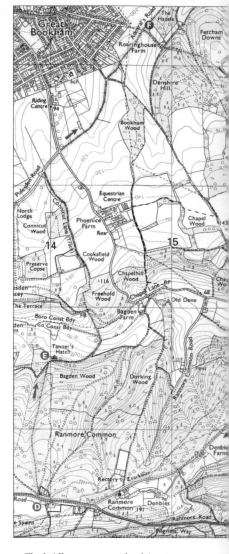.

This is a lovely stretch of a mile or so of woodland-walking and then the roof and chimneys of Polesden Lacey can be seen over a clearing to the left. The house becomes hidden as the track drops down to the picturesque youth hostel, Tanner's Hatch, where a bridleway joins from the left.

Pass the hostel and continue downhill along a delightful track which reaches the bottom of an open valley, where a bridle-way swings eastwards to the right. Walk along the track to pass beneath a balus-traded bridge carrying an estate road over the track. The climb is steep for a while through Freehold Wood.

Turn right onto Polesden Road, where there is a parallel bridleway on the left. Where Polesden Road meets a major road, cross straight over to walk up a track with a jumping-ground to the left. This track, known as Admiral's Road, skirts Great Bookham and once it has crossed another bridleway it becomes a field-edge path, narrow and enclosed for a short distance before meeting a track into Norbury Park.

Turn right onto this track ⑤ and go down the hill to pass Roaringhouse Farm. Keep straight on after the red-brick farmhouse up a bridleway which climbs steeply to start with and then descends abruptly. Keep straight on when a foot-path and then a track cross, and continue through a group of yews. The bridleway meets another track where there is no waymark. Bear left and walk along the track a short way to another junction ⑤ with a picnic-site, an information board about Norbury Park and a signpost. Bear left again here, following the direction to Mickleham.

The bridleway passes the drive to an elegant mansion, the home of Dr Marie Stopes at the time of her death in 1957. The bridleway joins the drive from the house, before leaving it to the right, by a seat. Another driveway is crossed and then the route follows the perimeter fence to a signpost on the right to a viewpoint ⑤. It is worth the short detour to visit this spot where a seat has been placed so that that the fine view southwards to Box Hill may be enjoyed in comfort. The viewpoint must be one of the few good things to have followed the 1987 hurricane, which opened up the vista.

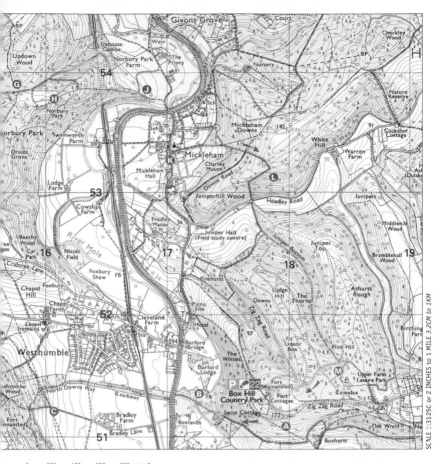

SCALE 1:31250 or 2 INCHES to 1 MILE 3.2CM to 1KM

0	200	400	600	800 METRES 1
				KILOMETRES
				MILES
0	200	400	600 YARDS	1/2

Returning to the bridleway, this descends steeply to reach a surfaced track. Ignore a bridleway sign to the right and remain on the track until it swings sharply to the left **J**. Keep straight on here on a narrow path. Turn right when the track meets a lane at the bottom, to cross a bridge over the River Mole to the main road. Take care when crossing this to the road opposite, which leads to Mickleham.

Turn left immediately past the church onto a driveway to Eastfield Cottage **K**. At a white gate take the footpath over the stile to the right. This path through the woods soon begins to climb. Note the remains of a wall of dressed flint on the right. Go straight over Mickleham Downs Road. At the top of the following climb,

the path swings to the right and begins to descend through a grove of yews. In the middle of these it swings right again **L** and then suddenly the view opens up ahead. There is a seat here. The path then begins a slippery descent to Juniper Bottom, or Happy Valley. Although steps have been cut for the latter part of the way, great care has to be taken initially, especially after wet weather. Cross the road at the bottom to enter Juniper Bottom.

The final part of the walk is through a valley flanked by rich woodland that gradually encroaches on the track as it climbs. Posts with numbers denote stages of a National Trust nature trail. Almost at the top of Juniper Bottom, at post 14 **M**, turn right to leave the bridleway. Level walking follows through the woods; you may see deer. Follow the nature trail posts with grey arrows back to the car park. ●

Bignor Hill and Stane Street (vertical, left margin)

Bignor Hill and Stane Street

Start	National Trust car park on Bignor Hill, at end of narrow lane about 1½ miles (2.4km) south-west of Bignor village
Distance	8 miles (12.9km). Shorter version 5½ miles (8.9km)
Approximate time	4 hours (3 hours for shorter version)
Parking	Bignor Hill
Refreshments	Pub at Sutton
Ordnance Survey maps	Landranger 197 (Chichester & The Downs), Explorer 121 (Arundel & Pulborough)

There is very much a Roman theme to this walk which passes close to a Roman villa and follows a stretch of the Roman Stane Street as it crosses the South Downs. In addition a number of superb viewpoints from the crest of the downs, two attractive villages nestling beneath them and areas of fine woodland make up a most varied and absorbing walk. There are quite a few 'ups and downs' but only one steep climb.

The finest view of the walk comes at the starting point on Bignor Hill, a magnificent vista southwards across woodland and downland. Begin by facing back along the lane and taking the grassy track that bears right off it, part of the South Downs Way. The track heads gently uphill between fields to the highest point on Bignor Hill, passes to the right of Toby's Stone, a memorial to a local huntsman, and then heads downhill, curving to the right. At a public footpath sign turn sharp left and continue more steeply downhill to a junction by a South Downs Way sign and just to the left of three barns **A**. Here turn left along a track (signposted 'Roman Villa'), head uphill into woodland and keep on the main track all the while as it winds through the trees, finally descending to a lane at a sharp bend **B**.

Keep ahead along the lane for nearly ½ mile (800m) into Bignor. At a T-junction turn right and almost immediately turn left (signposted Sutton

and Duncton) to walk through the small and attractive village. A detour of ¼ mile (400m) to the right, at a public footpath sign and by a most picturesque, timber-framed medieval house with an overhanging thatched roof, will bring you to Bignor Roman Villa which displays some of the finest mosaics in Britain, first discovered in 1811.

The route continues by following the lane around a left-hand bend, passing to the left of the restored medieval church. By the church turn left down another lane, then at a public footpath sign turn right **C** through a gate and walk across grass, below a house on the right, to pick up a path that passes into woodland. Cross a

footbridge over a stream and continue along an often muddy path made broad in places by walkers trying to avoid the mire. Turn left by a pond, cross another footbridge and continue over a third footbridge to a stile.

Climb it, keep ahead across a field to pass through a gap in a line of trees and continue uphill across the next field to climb another stile. Keep in a straight line across the middle of a field to a stile and a public footpath sign on the edge of Sutton **D**. To visit the village of Sutton, which

has a pub and a fine medieval church, bypass an overgrown stile and follow the enclosed path ahead; otherwise turn left along the right-hand edge of the field, by fences and hedges bordering gardens on the right, following the field edge as it curves first to the left and then to the right. In front there are fine views of the wooded slopes of the South Downs. Climb a stile, keep ahead across a paddock, climb

SCALE 1:27 777 or about 2¼ INCHES to 1 MILE 3.6CM to 1KM

Medieval house at Bignor

another stile and continue along the right-hand edge of a field, following this as it bears left in front of houses. Where the field-edge later bears right, continue straight ahead, in the direction of a public footpath sign, across the middle of the field to climb a stile and follow a downhill path through trees. Bear right to a public footpath sign on emerging from the trees, turn left, cross a stream and head diagonally uphill across a field to another public footpath sign in the top right-hand corner. Continue in the same direction across the next field towards a farm and at the far end of the field you join a lane.

Keep ahead along the lane, passing to the right of Glatting Farm, follow it around a left-hand bend and almost immediately turn right Ⓔ, at a public footpath sign. Walk across the middle of a field, bearing slightly right to pass through trees at the far end, cross a stream and continue in a straight line across a smaller field, heading up to a stile; climb it to enter woodland. Now comes the most difficult part of the walk, a steep climb along a narrow, winding and overgrown path up to a T-junction and public footpath sign Ⓕ. Here turn left along an easier and very attractive path just below the top edge of the wood. Keep to the right at a fork, and at a meeting of paths and

tracks bear left along a track to a T-junction a few yards after this.

Turn left along a broad track which heads steadily uphill over open downland, giving fine views over to the left, where both Sutton and Bignor can be seen below. After the National Trust sign for Bignor Hill and just in front of radio masts, a track leads off to the right Ⓖ.

If doing the shorter version of the walk, keep ahead here and the track leads directly back to the car park.

Turn right, keep ahead at a crossroads (crossing the South Downs Way) and just a few yards further on turn half-right, in the direction of a public bridleway sign, along a path by the right-hand edge of woodland. At a T-junction turn right along a track heading towards woodland and continue into the trees. In front of a Forestry Commission sign for Eartham Wood turn left Ⓗ, at a public bridleway sign, along a path that heads gently downhill through a most attractive area of woodland to reach a complex junction of eight different paths and a multitude of footpath signs Ⓙ.

Turn left along the path, signposted to Bignor, to join Stane Street, the Roman road that ran from London to Chichester. Much of it has vanished under tarmac – part of it is now the A29 – but this section is well-preserved with the 'agger' or raised surface and occasionally the small drainage ditches on either side still clearly visible.

Follow the line of this Roman road in a straight line back to the starting point, a grand finale to the walk. At first the path is pleasantly tree-lined, then it continues through more open country and later ascends to the crest of the downs with grand and sweeping views to the right. Finally keep along the left-hand edge of woodland to reach the car park where the much-photographed footpath sign in Latin reveals the Roman origins of this routeway. ●

Lewes, Balmer Down and the River Ouse

Start	Lewes
Distance	10 miles (16km)
Approximate time	5 hours
Parking	Lewes – Brook Street/Spring Gardens car park
Refreshments	Pubs and cafés at Lewes and Offham
Ordnance Survey maps	Landranger 198 (Brighton & The Downs), Explorer 122 (South Downs Way – Steyning to Newhaven)

The walk begins and ends at Lewes, a town with an abundance of old buildings, including a notable castle. Once out of the town, the way lies over tracts of lonely downland where the walking, though often energetic, cannot fail to be enjoyable.

Dominating the historic town of Lewes is the Norman castle. There are some fine medieval churches and a 16th-century house, now a museum, that was once the home of Anne of Cleves.

Turn right out of the car park and walk up North Street, bearing right into West Street which takes you to Mount Pleasant. Turn left up the hill opposite the Elephant and Castle pub to climb Castle Banks, heading towards Lewes Castle. On the left you pass the bowling-green where the game has been played since 1640 (before this it was a jousting-ground) and there are intriguing glimpses of the medieval fortifications. The most impressive of these is Castle Gate, the main entrance to the castle. Pass through this to emerge into the High Street and turn right.

At the top of the High Street, opposite the Pelham Arms and just before the church, turn left down Church Lane, a footpath which passes by the County Hall car park to reach Rotten Row. Turn right, then fork left down St Pancras Road and turn right at the end. Pass the Swan Inn and bear right Ⓐ down Jugg's Road, which

soon swings left to cross the bypass by a bridge. Once over the bridge, Jugg's Road begins to climb, with a good view of Lewes.

Soon the lane leads into open country, crossing unfenced fields. A track winds up a distant hill ahead – our objective after reaching Kingston. At Kingston Hollow cross directly over a lane onto a private road to Kingstonridge, an estate of 1930s housing. After leaving the last of these dwellings the track, still Jugg's Road, begins to climb steeply. The woods of Ashcombe Bottom can be seen on the northern horizon, beyond fields. The route skirts these woods before turning back towards Lewes. At the top keep straight on, with the fence on the right, and cross a stile.

The grassy track runs just below the ridge, heading towards a transmitter mast. However, well before reaching the mast, go through a gate next to a gas pumping station and immediately turn right to leave Jugg's Road Ⓑ, onto a bridleway heading north-west (South Downs Way). Falmer is seen ahead as the path drops down to Newmarket Plantation, where it swings to the right. Descend the track until you see a small gate to the left of a finger-post **C**. Branch left through the gate, following the South Downs Way. Go through a metal gate and descend steeply to a field-edge path with trees to the right. This goes below the railway line before turning left, parallel to the main road. It eventually joins a road leading up to a bridge crossing the A27. Turn right after the bridge to pass Housedean Farm, and at the end of the wall turn left to climb the steps to a gate. This bridleway soon takes you up Long Hill. The South Downs Way drops down through Bunkershill Plantation, and then emerges onto downland again. It veers right to begin a gentle climb to reach a gate and a junction with a footpath. Turn left here and climb over Balmer Down, across open, rolling countryside. The pylon at the top of the hill is in sight for about 2 miles (3.2km). Just beyond this a bridleway is met **D**: turn right onto it.

A level stretch follows on a good farm track. At a five-way junction **E** turn east to Lewes. Watch out for cyclists. The right-of-way follows the fence on the right, rather than diverting towards Blackcap, but it bears left after Blackcap to climb Mount Harry.

Continuing eastwards; keep the fence on the right and look for blue waymarks on posts. Gradually the bridleway turns towards the south and begins to descend. It leaves the fence to cross a field with a

pylon. Make for a gap in the trees ahead just to the left of the pylon, and then bear right off the main track to head for the edge of a wood – there is another pylon at this point. Skirt round the top of the wood; you will catch a glimpse of Offham

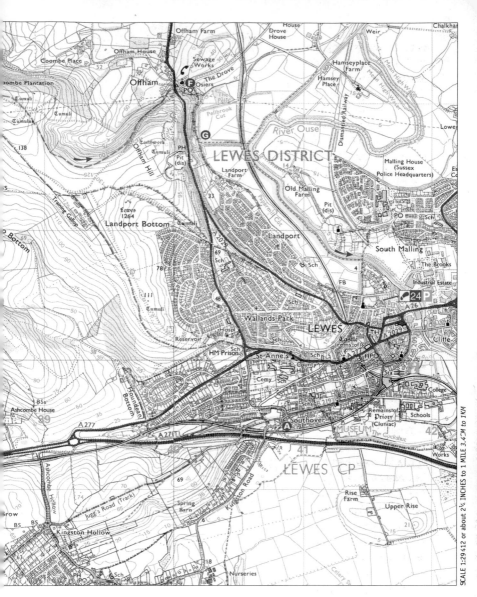

church through the trees. Go through a gate to a field-edge bridleway, still at the top of the wood. After about $^1/_2$ mile (800m) look for another blue-marked post which shows where the path enters the wood.

The shady downhill path leads to a gate and out of the wood onto a chalky track; a parallel track is even more deeply etched into the chalk. The track meets with the main road close to the pub at Offham.

Cross the main road to the lane to Hamsey and turn right off this at a bend **F**, before the Old Post House car park, onto a bridleway into a wood. Look for a stile on this side **G** which gives onto a grassy, embanked path to the railway. Pass beneath the railway and then cross two stiles to the river. Turn right and walk by the River Ouse back to Lewes. At the river footbridge, turn right, walk past the swimming-pool by an ornamental canal to Brook Street and turn left to the car park.

Friston Forest, the Seven Sisters and Cuckmere Haven

Friston Forest, the Seven Sisters and Cuckmere Haven

Start	Seven Sisters Country Park car park at Exceat
Distance	6½ miles (10.5km)
Approximate time	3½ hours
Parking	Exceat
Refreshments	Farm café at Exceat
Ordnance Survey maps	Landranger 199 (Eastbourne & Hastings), Explorer 123 (South Downs Way – Newhaven to Eastbourne)

SCALE 1:26316 or about 2½ INCHES to 1 MILE 3.8CM to 1KM

Forest, downs, coast and river combine to create a most satisfying and superbly varied walk. A pleasant ramble along wide, green tracks through the woodlands of Friston Forest is followed by a walk across smooth and open downland to reach the coast. Then comes the scenic highlight and most strenuous part of the route: a series of quite steep climbs over four of the Seven Sisters, the succession of chalk cliffs (there are actually eight) that lie just to the west of Beachy Head and one of the most spectacular stretches of coastline in England. After Cuckmere Haven, a gentle stroll by the meandering River Cuckmere makes a relaxing finale.

Nowadays Exceat is little more than a name on a map and a few farm buildings by a bridge over the River Cuckmere; the village was abandoned after the Black Death and a series of French raids. Its remains and the site of the church lie buried under fields. An 18th-century converted barn serves as a visitor centre for the Seven Sisters Country Park, which covers the area of downland, river, estuary and coast to the south. Next door to this is a fascinating 'Living World' exhibition, containing many rare insects.

Turn right out of the car park along the main road and take the first track on the left, at a South Downs Way sign. Climb a stile, bear slightly right and head uphill across a field to go through a gate, immediately climbing a stone stile in a wall to enter Friston Forest, a delightful area of mixed woodland managed by the Forestry Commission. Take the path signposted to Westdean through the trees, descending via a long flight of steps into the sleepy and unspoilt village. Turn right along a lane **A**, at a public bridleway sign to Friston and Jevington. Just before reaching a Friston Forest sign, a short detour to the left brings you to the small, plain church with the short tower and spire typical of Sussex.

Keep ahead along the lane, heading uphill into woodland again, where the tarmac lane becomes a forest track. Now follow this lovely, broad, grassy track for nearly 1½ miles (2.4km) through the forest. At a fork take the right-hand uphill track, in the Friston direction, and later, where the roughly made-up forest track veers left, go ahead on a grassy path.

The spectacular Seven Sisters – where the South Downs meet the sea

Descend to cross a track, continue uphill again, keeping along the right-hand edge of an area of open grassland, and finally head downhill to pass beside a barrier onto a tarmac drive Ⓑ.

Turn left and, where the drive bends right, keep ahead along a track to a footpath sign just in front of a barrier. Turn right, in the Friston direction, along a path that runs parallel to the tarmac drive on the right. At a yellow waymarked public footpath sign turn right, following directions to Friston and East Dean, up steps and through a gate. Keep straight ahead across a field, go through a gate on the far side and descend steps to a tarmac drive. Cross it, bear slightly left to climb the stile opposite and continue diagonally and slightly uphill across a field to another stile in the far corner. Climb it and follow a path through woodland, finally climbing a stone stile on the left to reach the main road at a junction Ⓒ.

Cross the road and take the tarmac track opposite (signposted 'Crowlink, no through road'), passing between a lily pond on the right and Friston's small, attractive church on the left. The tarmac track soon becomes a rough track. Just before entering the National Trust's Crowlink car park, turn left through a gate and then turn half-right to follow the direction of the yellow – not the blue – waymark diagonally across a field. Go through a gate and bear right along a rather indistinct path Ⓓ, keeping in a straight line diagonally across the field. Although the numerous paths across this National Trust property may appear confusing, there is no problem; once you reach the brow of a hill, simply make for the prominent group of farm buildings seen below. Look out for a stile in a wire fence, climb it and continue downhill to pass through a hedge gap onto a track.

Turn left along the track, passing to the left of the farm buildings, go through a gate and walk through the dry valley of Gap Bottom, keeping by a wire fence and hedge on the right. Continue along a wide, smooth, grassy path that winds through the shallow valley bottom to the edge of the cliffs Ⓔ.

Turn right onto the South Downs Way to Cuckmere Haven, a route that climbs over four of the series of chalk cliffs known as the Seven Sisters. There are some steep 'ups and downs' on this section but the superb cliff scenery and the magnificent, extensive views more than compensate for the effort expended. Over the last brow you look down on Cuckmere Haven, the beautiful and unspoilt estuary of the Cuckmere, with its shingle beach, lagoons and meandering river, and beyond that to Seaford Head.

Descend steeply towards the beach and just before the final, steep descent, turn right over a stile and along the side of the valley above the river. Head downhill along a pleasant, grassy path, go through a gate and bear right. At a T-junction of tracks bear right, go through a gate and continue along a concrete track to the right of the marshes, lagoons and meanders of the Cuckmere, among the finest river meanders in Britain. In 1846 this section of the river was straightened and canalised to reduce flooding. As you near Exceat, bear left onto a grassy track, back to the car park. ●

Ditchling Beacon and Wolstonbury Hill

Ditchling Beacon and Wolstonbury Hill

Start	Ditchling Beacon
Distance	9½ miles (15.3km). Shorter version 5½ miles (8.9km)
Approximate time	4 hours (3 hours for shorter version)
Parking	National Trust car park at Ditchling Beacon
Refreshments	Pubs at Pyecombe and Clayton
Ordnance Survey maps	Landranger 198 (Brighton & The Downs), Explorer 122 (South Downs Way – Steyning to Newhaven)

This is a remarkably enjoyable walk that takes in three superb viewpoints and also manages to cover meadow and woodland paths threading through delightful countryside and villages. Ditchling Beacon is highly popular with the public as it has a car park more or less at its summit. The two windmills (which feature on the shorter version but may be visited by detouring from the longer one) also attract a lot of visitors, but in contrast Wolstonbury Hill lies further off the beaten track, and here one can best appreciate the beguiling character of a downland landscape. The shorter version omits Wolstonbury Hill.

The National Trust car park at the start of this walk provides a wonderful view to the north over Burgess Hill and Haywards Heath towards Ashdown Forest. Climb the stile at the top of the car park and take the chalky track which climbs southwards. A path to the left leads to the Beacon itself and the triangulation pillar, but ignore this and continue a little further to find a stile on the left **Ⓐ** by a Sussex Wildlife Trust information board. The signpost shows this to be a blue route going to Heathy Brow. From this point the view northwards is even more spectacular than from the car park and will be enjoyed again on the final leg of the walk.

The path heads south from the stile and soon gives a marvellous vista down Hogtrough Bottom – a dry valley popular with paragliders. An alternative path from

the Beacon joins from the left and then the bridleway begins to descend to cross the head of another dry valley, Heathy Brow. Go through the gate ahead and then bear right, heading for Lower Standean through a lovely valley. In the distance the A23 can be seen climbing a steep escarpment towards Brighton. On a good day the sea can be seen sparkling beyond.

North Bottom is a beautiful meadow scattered with ash and hawthorn trees. At the bottom, pass through a gate on the right and then bear left to continue along the valley, branching right after 200 yds (183m) onto a track which climbs the right side of the valley. After an initial steep climb, a gate comes into view ahead and after this the track dips down again as it approaches Lower Standean.

The track meets another bridleway on

the west side of the farm-yard **B**, where there is a prominent signpost. Turn right and continue up the track, heading for a farm building of flint and brick which stands alone in a large meadow. After this the track passes through a gap in the hedge and zigzags by hedges up to the top of the rise. The West Sussex Border Path crosses here. Keep straight on along the field edge. The Clayton windmills come into view, and the bridleway leaves the hedge to swing west **C**; about 100 yds (91m) after this turn right onto a newly diverted track **D**. The windmills are soon in view again as the bridleway – a chalky, flinty track – heads west, skirting the boundary of Pyecombe golf-course.

Those wishing to do the shorter version should keep straight on when the South Downs Way meets our route **E**, *to pass New Barn Farm and heading for the windmills. Turn left onto the track beyond the farm if you wish to visit the windmills. Otherwise turn right onto the track which climbs steadily to rejoin the main route at the top* **L**.

Continue to walk down the track by the golf-course, which eventually reaches the main road just to the east of Pyecombe village. Cross the road to a bridleway which runs parallel to it, on the other side of a hedge. Turn right down School Lane towards Pyecombe church but, before reaching the church, turn sharp right up a track called The Wycke **F**. If you wish to visit Pyecombe, keep ahead to pass the church, which contains a unique Norman font made of lead and intricately decorated. There is a pub at the end of Church Lane. The Wycke soon narrows into a muddy and rather overgrown

bridleway. After a short distance the nettles improve but in wet weather the mud gets worse. Keep straight on when a footpath crosses but, on meeting another bridleway, cross the track to a small gate **G** just beyond the signpost on the left. This gives access to Wolstonbury Hill, National Trust land which quickly proves to be an outstanding viewpoint. Downland walking is at its best here, on close-cropped turf.

Near the top, where the view has opened up to the north, there is a gate. Continue down the track for another 100 yds (91m) – now there are views westwards too – and turn right at the signpost to climb to the summit. The view from the triangulation pillar **H** embraces 360° and a considerable area of southern England. The main path on Wolstonbury Hill follows the ramparts of the prehistoric fort. Return to the point on these where the path left for the summit, and take the steep path down heading towards Clayton, making directly for the large white house on the main road. Climb a stile and continue descending on the footpath

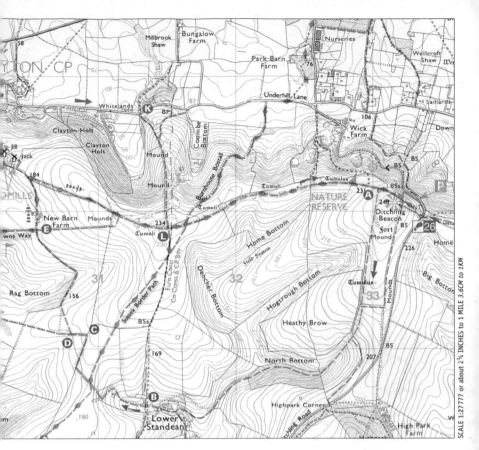

which crosses a large meadow on a slightly raised bank, skirting a pit on the right. At the bottom there is a gate and stile **J**: turn left after these onto a chalky track which runs through Ashen Plantation. Ignore a branching footpath to the left and keep on the main track, passing a cottage ('Warenne') before reaching a lane, where you turn right. This quiet byway takes us to the main road at Clayton; the pub is on the left.

Turn right to the bridge over the railway, pausing to view the remarkable tunnel portal. Castellated turrets flank a cottage perched above the rails. Cross the road after the bridge to Underhill Lane, which leads past the recreation ground and Clayton church. The latter is dedicated to St John the Baptist and is notable for its superb wall-paintings depicting the Last Judgment, which probably date from around 1080. The lovely interior of the

church has altered little in 900 years.

Carry on down the lane for about 1 mile (1.6km). It is a delightful byway, rarely disturbed by much traffic as it winds past beautiful old buildings before striking eastwards below the wooded slopes of Clayton Holt. Just beyond Whitelands Farm on the left, the lane bends to the left and begins to climb. At this point **K** take the bridleway to the right and climb the steep path through the trees. After a short distance the track joins an easier, surfaced track which continues to climb. Finally the bridleway becomes grassy, and soon after this the summit of the down is reached **L**, and the shorter route joins from the right. The view to the north is a fitting reward for the exertion.

Pass through the gate and turn left to enjoy an exhilarating finale to the walk along the narrow ridge which leads back to Ditchling Beacon. ●

Frensham Common
and Kettlebury Hill

Start	Frensham Little Pond
Distance	8 miles (12.9km)
Approximate time	4 hours
Parking	National Trust car park at Frensham Little Pond
Refreshments	None
Ordnance Survey maps	Landranger 186 (Aldershot & Guildford), Explorers 133 (Haslemere & Petersfield) and 145 (Guildford & Farnham)

There can be few walks which better illustrate the varied nature of Surrey's landscape than this one. At the beginning and end there is pleasant walking in coppiced woodland, while the middle section goes through an area of forestry reminiscent of parts of Scotland. Much of the return leg, along the ridge of Kettlebury Hill, gives wide views northwards to Guildford and beyond.

From the car park walk eastwards along the road until a footpath leaves on the right to skirt the pond. As the path winds its way through pine trees it is hard to imagine a more pleasant way to start a walk. Where the path meets a fence on the left Ⓐ follow this out of the National Trust land. The path becomes a track between fields, with a fence to the left and a tree nursery to the right.

Keep straight on over another track – there are now pine woods to the right and a field on the left. At the end of this field Ⓑ turn sharp right onto a bridleway. This soon meets a road: turn right onto this, which passes through murky swampland. Cross the ford (there is a footbridge) and immediately after this Ⓒ leave the road by bearing left to follow the blue waymark of a bridleway. After Grey Walls Ⓓ turn left onto another bridleway (number 42), and keep on this main track to pass to the rear of Lowicks House with its large pond.

Turn left where a metal bridleway sign points straight on Ⓔ so that a paddock is to the left. The sandy track descends past the driveway to Crosswater House; after this it becomes surfaced.

Continue on this lane to pass a cattery and then Crosswater Mill on the right, and turn left after these onto a track to Tanglewood, bridleway P5 Ⓕ. This leads into an area known as the Flashes, a heathery basin which would not be out of place in the Scottish Highlands. The track enters woods again, having skirted this area of emptiness (though since it has been replanted with conifers its character may soon be lost). It passes a drive to a house on the right and after this, another track leaves on the left. Ignore this and keep on bridleway P5.

The Devil's Jumps, four Bronze Age tombs dating from around 500 BC, can be seen in the meadow to the right, just before the track meets a junction of five tracks. Again keep straight on, staying with P5.

Houses can now be seen on top of the hill ahead, and soon after this the track meets the road on the outskirts of Rushmoor **G**. Turn left and then after 100 yds (91m) turn right down a track leading to a military training area. Cross a stream, turn left onto the track beyond it and then right at the next junction, also of five tracks. Bear left when the track divides **H** – the views improve as height is gained – and carry straight on over the next junction, climbing steeply to reach

the bridleway on the crest of Kettlebury Hill **J**. Turn left onto this.

The army have firing ranges close by so the sound of gunfire may startle you here, as it does the numerous deer which graze the hill. For all this, the walking is delightful on top of the sandy ridge. Bear right to keep to the crest when another bridleway leaves to the left. Look for the distinctive shape of Guildford Cathedral to the north at the next junction, which for

SCALE 1:29412 or about 2¼ INCHES to 1 MILE 3.4CM to 1KM

some reason is known as Lion's Mouth **K**. There is a meeting of five ways on the top of the ridge: go left and descend to another bridleway sign, where this time seven paths meet.

Turn half-left onto bridleway 101 (as shown by a short post with an arrow). After about 220 yds (200m), at cross tracks, go straight across onto a track through Hankley Common golf-course. It is ¼ mile (400m), just after passing between two golf greens, to more crosstracks, marked by another post with an arrow **L**. Turn right and keep on this track – ignoring all tracks off to left and right – and cross a short golf hole, then two fairways, for another ¼ mile (400m). From here on the track rises gently through open pine and heathland for nearly ¼ mile (400m) to a track that slants across the one you are on. Go straight across and on for 200 yds (183m) to a junction of six tracks **M**. Take the first track to the left which leads towards a plantation, descending gradually. Tracks join from the left and then, in a clearing, from the right. Keep straight on; the bridleway drops more steeply as it nears Stockbridge Pond and skirts the northern end of this before reaching the road, where there is a car park **N**.

Cross the road and take the track on the other side bearing the red 'HR' waymark. Go left after 400 yds (366m) when the track divides and enjoy this lovely, undemanding end to a walk which has covered some of the best of Surrey's countryside. The leafy track emerges directly opposite the car park at Frensham Little Pond. ●

Frensham Common – pleasant walking country

Cissbury and Chanctonbury Rings

Start	Findon Valley. Leave Worthing on the A24 and turn right into Lime Tree Avenue, just before the Esso filling station. Fork right up Coombe Rise to the car park at the top
Distance	10½ miles (16.9km)
Approximate time	5½ hours
Parking	Findon Valley car park
Refreshments	None
Ordnance Survey maps	Landranger 198 (Brighton & The Downs), Explorer 121 (Arundel & Pulborough)

This lengthy walk of broad and sweeping vistas not only embraces some of the grandest scenery on the South Downs but also passes two of the finest prehistoric hill forts – Cissbury Ring and Chanctonbury Ring. Although there are several climbs, these are all long and gradual.

Begin by taking the uphill track from the car park, at a fork keep along the right-hand path, go through a gate and continue uphill to a T-junction of paths **Ⓐ**. Turn left along a pleasantly hedge- and tree-lined path, eventually emerging into open country, with a fine view of Cissbury Ring straight ahead. Go through a gate at a public bridleway sign, keep ahead past a second footpath sign and continue along the left-hand edge of a copse lined by some fine old trees, to a gate and National Trust sign for Cissbury Ring.

Go through the gate to pass through the ramparts of this huge fort, one of the greatest of Iron Age hill forts, enclosing an area of 65 acres (26.3 ha). The inner bank has a circumference of over 1 mile (1.6km). Built around 300 BC, the fort was deserted sometime between 50 BC and AD 50 but reinforced and reoccupied after the departure of the Romans; whether this

was done by the Saxons or by the Britons as a defence against the Saxons is uncertain.

Continue along a broad grassy track and about 100 yds (91m) before reaching a triangulation pillar, where the track bears slightly right, the route bears left along a narrower grassy track. However, it is worth while to continue to the triangulation pillar (604ft (184m)) for the magnificent views from it. These extend along a great length of the Sussex coast from Beachy Head to the Isle of Wight, and inland across the downs towards the Weald, with the circle of beeches that crown Chanctonbury Ring clearly visible to the north.

After bearing left onto the narrower track follow it downhill, pass over the ramparts, go down some steps and over a stile at a public footpath sign, and continue more steeply downhill to a gate and National Trust sign at the bottom **Ⓑ**. Go through the gate, turn right along a

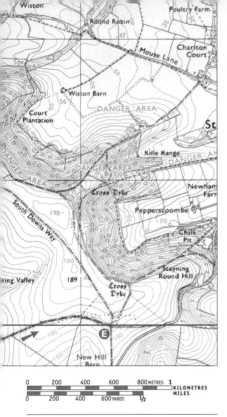

```
0      200    400    600    800 METRES  1
                                        KILOMETRES
                                        MILES
0      200    400    600 YARDS   ½
```

Continue along the South Downs Way, passing below the triangulation pillar on Chanctonbury Hill – 780ft (238m) high and another superb viewpoint – and to the left of a restored dew-pond, first made in around 1870 to provide water for animals. Head gently downhill and where the South Downs Way turns right keep straight ahead, continuing downhill all the while. At a crossing of tracks turn left **G**, continuing downhill at first but soon starting to head uphill. Look out for a bridleway sign which directs you through a gate on the right.

Keep in a straight line across a field to go through a metal gate onto a lane, cross over, go through a gate opposite and continue gently uphill across the next field, keeping in the same direction as before, to a gate. Go through it to a crossing of tracks, turn left and pass to the left of a house, after which the track narrows to a hedge- and tree-lined path. Continue along it, keeping ahead at the first public bridleway sign, but at a T-junction bear left onto a broad track.

Continue along this track for about 100 yds (91m), passing one public bridle-way sign and turning right **H** at the second one at a crossing of tracks. The track leads straight to Cissbury Ring where you pick up the outward route **B** and retrace your steps through the fort back to the start.   ●

Looking from Cissbury Ring towards the circle of beeches that crown Chanctonbury Ring

broad stony track which heads gently downhill and continue, between wire fences, to a public bridleway sign **C**.

Here turn left along a track that winds through Stump Bottom and at a T-junction **D** turn right onto a path that at first heads steadily uphill and later flattens out. Ignore a public footpath sign to the left and continue to a crossing of paths and tracks; here turn left to join the South Downs Way **E**. Follow it gently uphill for 2 miles (3.2km), ignoring all side turns, to Chanctonbury Ring **F**, another Iron Age fort but much smaller than Cissbury Ring. It is easily distinguished by its circle of beeches, planted in the 1760s by Charles Goring, a local landowner, which gives the fort an air of mystery, especially in misty conditions. In clear weather there is a magnificent view across the wide, empty expanses of the downs looking south-wards towards Cissbury Ring and the coast.

Further Information

 ### The National Trust

Anyone who likes visiting places of natural beauty and/or historic interest has cause to be grateful to the National Trust. Without it, many such places would probably have vanished by now.

It was in response to the pressures on the countryside posed by the relentless march of Victorian industrialisation that the trust was set up in 1895. Its founders, inspired by the common goals of protecting and conserving Britain's national heritage and widening public access to it, were Sir Robert Hunter, Octavia Hill and Canon Rawnsley: respectively a solicitor, a social reformer and a clergyman. The latter was particularly influential. As a canon of Carlisle Cathedral and vicar of Crosthwaite (near Keswick), he was concerned about threats to the Lake District and had already been active in protecting footpaths and promoting public access to open countryside. After the flooding of Thirlmere in 1879 to create a large reservoir, he became increasingly convinced that the only effective way to guarantee protection was outright ownership of land.

The purpose of the National Trust is to preserve areas of natural beauty and sites of historic interest by acquisition, holding them in trust for the nation and making them available for public access and enjoyment. Some of its properties have been acquired through purchase, but many have come to the Trust as donations. Nowadays, it is not only one of the biggest landowners in the country, but also one of the most active conservation charities, protecting 581,113 acres (253,176 ha) of land, including 555 miles (892km) of coastline, and over 300 historic properties in England, Wales and Northern Ireland. (There is a separate National Trust for Scotland, which was set up in 1931.)

Furthermore, once a piece of land has come under National Trust ownership, it is difficult for its status to be altered. As a result of parliamentary legislation in 1907, the Trust was given the right to declare its property inalienable, so ensuring that in any subsequent dispute it can appeal directly to parliament.

As it works towards its dual aims of conserving areas of attractive countryside and encouraging greater public access (not easy to reconcile in this age of mass tourism), the Trust provides an excellent service for walkers by creating new concessionary paths and waymarked trails, maintaining stiles and footbridges and combating the ever-increasing problem of footpath erosion.

For details of membership, contact the National Trust at the address on page 94.

 ### The Ramblers' Association

No organisation works more actively to protect and extend the rights and interests of walkers in the countryside than the Ramblers' Association. Its aims are clear: to foster a greater knowledge, love and care of the countryside; to assist in the protection and enhancement of public rights of way and areas of natural beauty; to work for greater public access to the countryside; and to encourage more people to take up rambling as a healthy, recreational leisure activity.

It was founded in 1935 when, following the setting up of a National Council of Ramblers' Federations in 1931, a number of federations earlier formed in London, Manchester, the Midlands and elsewhere came together to create a more effective pressure group, to deal with such problems as the disappearance and obstruction of footpaths, the prevention of access to open mountain and moorland and increasing hostility from landowners. This was the era of the mass trespasses, when there were sometimes violent confrontations between ramblers and gamekeepers, especially on the moorlands of the Peak District.

Since then the Ramblers' Association has played an influential role in preserving and developing the national footpath network, supporting the creation of national parks and encouraging the designation and waymarking of long-distance routes.

Our freedom to walk in the countryside is precarious and requires constant vigilance. As well as the perennial problems of footpaths being illegally obstructed, disappearing through lack of use or extinguished by housing or road construction, new dangers can spring up at any time.

It is to meet such problems and dangers that the Ramblers' Association exists and represents the interests of all walkers. The address to write to for information on the Ramblers' Association and how to become a member is given on page 94.

Walkers and the Law

The average walker in a national park or other popular walking area, armed with the appropriate Ordnance Survey map, reinforced perhaps by a guidebook giving detailed walking instructions, is unlikely to run into legal difficulties, but it is useful to know something about the law relating to public rights of way. The right to walk over certain parts of the countryside has developed over a long period, and how such rights came into being is a complex subject, too lengthy to be discussed here. The following comments are intended simply as a helpful guide, backed up by the Countryside Access Charter, a concise summary of walkers' rights and obligations drawn up by the Countryside Agency (see page 94).

Basically there are two main kinds of public rights of way: footpaths (for walkers only) and bridleways (for walkers, riders on horseback and pedal cyclists). Footpaths and bridleways are shown by broken green lines on Ordnance Survey Pathfinder and Outdoor Leisure maps and broken red lines on Landranger maps. There is also a third category, called byways: chiefly broad tracks (green lanes) or farm roads, which walkers, riders and cyclists have to share, usually only occasionally, with motor vehicles. Many of these public paths have been in existence for hundreds of years and some even originated as prehistoric trackways and have been in constant use for well

Fine cliff scenery just to the east of Hastings

over 2000 years. Ways known as RUPPs (roads used as public paths) still appear on some maps. The legal definition of such byways is ambiguous and they are gradually being reclassified as footpaths, bridleways or byways.

The term 'right of way' means exactly what it says. It gives right of passage over what, in the vast majority of cases, is private land, and you are required to keep to the line of the path and not stray on to the land on either side. If you inadvertently wander off the right of way – either because of faulty map-reading or because the route is not clearly indicated on the ground – you are technically trespassing and the wisest course is to ask the nearest available person (farmer or fellow walker) to direct you back to the correct route. There are stories about unpleasant confrontations between walkers and farmers at times, but in general most farmers are co-operative when responding to a genuine and polite request for assistance in route-finding.

The church and pond at Hascombe – one of Surrey's many attractive villages

Obstructions can sometimes be a problem and probably the most common of these is where a path across a field has been ploughed up. It is legal for a farmer to plough up a path provided that he restores it within two weeks, barring exceptionally bad weather. This does not always happen and here the walker is presented with a dilemma: to follow the line of the path, even if this inevitably means treading on crops, or to walk around the edge of the field. The latter course of action often seems the best but this means that you would be trespassing and not keeping to the exact line of the path. In the case of other obstructions which may block a path (illegal fences and locked gates etc), common sense has to be used in order to negotiate them by the easiest method – detour or removal. You should only ever remove as much as is

necessary to get through, and if you can easily go round the obstruction without causing any damage, then you should do so. If you have any problems negotiating rights of way, you should report the matter to the rights of way department of the relevant council, which will take action with the landowner concerned.

Apart from rights of way enshrined by law, there are a number of other paths available to walkers. Permissive or concessionary paths have been created where a landowner has given permission for the public to use a particular route across his land. The main problem with these is that, as they have been granted as a concession, there is no legal right to use them and therefore they can be extinguished at any time. In practice, many of these concessionary routes have been established on land owned either by large public bodies such as the Forestry Commission, or by a private one, such as the National Trust, and as these mainly encourage walkers to use their paths, they are unlikely to be closed unless a change of ownership occurs.

Walkers also have free access to country parks (except where requested to keep away from certain areas for ecological reasons, e.g. wildlife protection,

Countryside Access Charter

Your rights of way are:

- public footpaths – on foot only. Sometimes waymarked in yellow
- bridleways – on foot, horseback and pedal cycle. Sometimes waymarked in blue
- byways (usually old roads), most 'roads used as public paths' and, of course, public roads – all traffic has the right of way

Use maps, signs and waymarks to check rights of way. Ordnance Survey Explorer and Landranger maps show most public rights of way

On rights of way you can:

- take a pram, pushchair or wheelchair if practicable
- take a dog (on a lead or under close control)
- take a short route round an illegal obstruction or remove it sufficiently to get past

You have a right to go for recreation to:

- public parks and open spaces – on foot
- most commons near older towns and cities – on foot and sometimes on horseback
- private land where the owner has a formal agreement with the local authority

In addition you can use the following by local or established custom or consent, but ask for advice if you are unsure:

- many areas of open country, such as moorland, fell and coastal areas, especially those in the care of the National Trust, and some commons
- some woods and forests, especially those owned by the Forestry Commission
- country parks and picnic sites
- most beaches
- canal towpaths
- some private paths and tracks Consent sometimes extends to horse-riding and cycling

For your information:

- county councils and London boroughs maintain and record rights of way, and register commons
- obstructions, dangerous animals, harassment and misleading signs on rights of way are illegal and you should report them to the county council
- paths across fields can be ploughed, but must normally be reinstated within two weeks
- landowners can require you to leave land to which you have no right of access
- motor vehicles are normally permitted only on roads, byways and some 'roads used as public paths'

Further Information

woodland regeneration, safeguarding of rare plants etc), canal towpaths and most beaches. By custom, though not by right, you may generally walk across the open and uncultivated higher land of mountain, moorland and fell, but this varies from area to area and from one season to another – grouse moors, for example, will be out of bounds during the breeding and shooting seasons and some open areas are used as Ministry of Defence firing ranges, so access will be restricted. In some areas the situation has been clarified as a result of 'access agreements' between the land-owners and either the county council or the national park authority, which clearly define when and where you can walk over such open country.

Walking Safety

Although the reasonably gentle country-side that is the subject of this book offers no real dangers to walkers at any time of the year, it is still advisable to take sensible precautions and follow certain well-tried guidelines.

Always take with you both warm and waterproof clothing and sufficient food and drink. Wear suitable footwear, such as strong walking-boots or shoes that give a good grip over stony ground, on slippery slopes and in muddy conditions. Try to obtain a local weather forecast and bear it in mind before you start. Do not be afraid to abandon your proposed route and return to your starting point in the event of a sudden and unexpected deterioration in the weather.

All the walks described in this book will be safe to do, given due care and respect, even during the winter. Indeed, a crisp, fine winter day often provides perfect walking conditions, with firm ground underfoot and a clarity that is not possible to achieve at any other time of the year.

The most difficult hazard likely to be encountered is mud, especially when walking along woodland and field paths, farm tracks and bridleways – the latter in particular can often get churned up by cyclists and horses. In summer, an additional difficulty may be narrow and overgrown paths, particularly along the edges of cultivated fields. Neither should constitute a major problem provided that the appropriate footwear is worn.

Useful Organisations

Council for the Protection of Rural England
128 Southwark Street,
London SE1 0SW
Tel. 020 7981 2800

Countryside Agency
John Dower House,
Crescent Place, Cheltenham,
Gloucestershire GL50 3RA.
Tel. 01242 521381

Forestry Commission
Information Branch,
231 Corstorphine Road,
Edinburgh EH12 7AT.
Tel. 0131 334 0303
Forest Enterprise
South East England District Office,
Bucks Horn Oak,
Farnham, Surrey GU10 4LS.
Tel. 01420 23666

Long Distance Walkers' Association
Bank House, High Street
Wrotham, Seven Oaks
Kent TN15 7AE
Tel. 01732 883705

National Trust
Membership and general enquiries:
PO Box 39, Bromley,
Kent BR1 3XL.
Tel. 020 8131 51111
Southern Regional Office:
Polesden Lacey, Dorking,
Surrey RH5 6BD.
Tel. 01372 453401
Kent & East Sussex Regional Office:
Scotney Castle,
Lamberhurst,
Tunbridge Wells,
Kent TN3 8JN.
Tel. 01892 890651

Ordnance Survey
Romsey Road, Maybush,
Southampton SO16 4GU.
Tel. 08456 05 05 05 (Lo-call)

Ramblers' Association
2nd Floor, Camelford House,
87–90 Albert Embankment,
London SE1 7TW
Tel. 020 7339 8500

Society of Sussex Downsmen
10 The Drive,
Hove, East Sussex
BN3 2JA.
Tel. 01273 771906

South-East England Tourist Board
The Old Brew House,
Warwick Park,
Tunbridge Wells,
Kent TN2 5TU.
Tel. 01892 540766

Local tourist information numbers
*(*not open all year):*
Aldershot: 01252 320968
Arundel: 01903 882268
Battle: 01424 773721
Bexhill-on-Sea: 01424 732208
Bognor Regis: 01243 823140
Brighton: 01273 292599
Chichester: 01243 775888
Eastbourne: 01323 411400
Fontwell: 01243 543269
Guildford: 01483 444333
*Hastings: 01424 781133

Horsham: 01403 211661
Lewes: 01273 483448
Midhurst: 01730 817322
Rye: 01797 226696
Seaford: 01323 897426
Worthing: 01903 210022

Youth Hostels Association
Trevelyan House,
Dimple Road, Matlock,
Derbyshire DE4 3YH
Tel. 01629 592600 (General enquiries)
Website: www.yha.org.uk

Ordnance Survey Maps of Surrey and Sussex

Surrey and Sussex are covered by Ordnance Survey 1:50 000 (1¼ inches to 1 mile or 2cm to 1km) scale Landranger map sheets 186, 187, 188, 189, 197, 198 and 199. These all-purpose maps are packed with information to help you explore the area. Viewpoints, picnic sites, places of interest, caravan and camping sites are shown, as well as public rights-of-way information such as footpaths and bridleways.

To examine Surrey and Sussex in more detail, and especially if you are planning walks, Ordnance Survey Explorer maps at 1:25 000 (2½ inches to 1 mile or 4cm to 1km) are ideal:

120 Chichester
121 Arundel & Pulborough
122 South Downs Way – Steyning to Newhaven
123 South Downs Way – Newhaven to Eastbourne
124 Hastings & Bexhill
125 Romney Marsh, Rye & Winchelsea
133 Haslemere & Petersfield
134 Crawley & Horsham
135 Ashdown Forest
136 The Weald, Royal Tunbridge Wells
145 Guildford & Farnham
146 Dorking, Box Hill & Reigate

To get to Surrey and Sussex use the Ordnance Survey Great Britain Route-planner at 1:625 000 (1 inch to 10 miles or 1cm to 6.25km) scale.

Ordnance Survey maps and guides are available from most booksellers, stationers and newsagents.

Autumn at Gibbet Hill – a famous viewpoint

www.totalwalking.co.uk

www.totalwalking.co.uk
is the official website of the Jarrold
Pathfinder and Short Walks guides. This
interactive website features a wealth of
information for walkers – from the latest
news on route diversions and advice from
professional walkers to product news,
free sample walks and promotional offers.

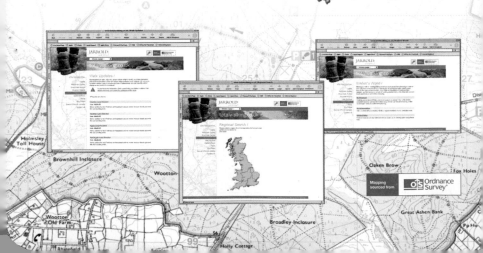